EXPERIENCES WITH THE DYING AND THE DEAD

EXPERIENCES WITH THE DYING AND THE DEAD

Waking to Our Connections with Those Who Have Died

CLAIRE BLATCHFORD

Blessings!
Claire

LINDISFARNE BOOKS
2007

Lindisfarne Books
www.lindisfarne.org
An Imprint of Anthroposophic Press, Inc.
610 Main Street, Suite 1
Great Barrington, MA 01230

BOOK DESIGN: WILLIAM JENS JENSEN

Printed on Recycled Paper

LIBRARY OF CONGRESS CATALOGING-IN-PUBLICATION DATA

Blatchford, Claire H.
  Experiences with the dying and the dead : waking to our
connections with those who have died / Claire Blatchford.
    p. cm.
  ISBN 978-1-58420-042-0
  1. Death. 2. Terminally ill. 3. Dreams. 4. Visions. I. Title.
  BD444.B555 2007
  155.9'37—dc22

                                              2007007836

CONTENTS

Foreword   vii

PART I: FIRST AWAKENINGS

When Children Die   2

A Startling Experience   10

A Death in the Family   13

My Grandmother's Journey   16

A True Physician   19

Connections Made through the Written Word   26

Barbara and Tim   32

Suicide   37

Annabelle   44

The Fire of Cancer   47

Another Death in the Family   55

The Night Watchman   61

PART II: JOHN

A Few Thoughts before the Next Story   68

John on This Side   71

John on the Other Side   89

AFTERWORD   109

SUGGESTED READING   121

*For John F. Gardner and Christopher Bamford
Dear friends, there and here,
who make so much possible.*

ℰℐ

*With appreciation to all who contributed
to the publication of this book.*

FOREWORD

HELEN KELLER SAID, "Blindness cuts one off from things, deafness cuts one off from people." Apart from a three-day ordeal when I was unable to see because of an injury to my cornea, I haven't experienced the full truth of what she said about blindness. As for deafness, I've been profoundly deaf in both ears for over fifty years and know very well what she means about being cut off from people.

For example, my husband listens to the news on the radio and though I can, through my hearing aid, hear sounds coming from it, they are, for me, no more than a rumble and a jumble. Or I attend a meeting at work and my coworkers, though they have no intention of leaving me out of the banter, laugh at a joke that flies right over my head. By the time someone has repeated what was said, another joke has come and gone. Or there are the occasions when I know a person has spoken to me and I simply can't "get it." I see the puzzled or annoyed expression on this person's face, but no matter how many times he repeats himself the topic eludes me, and if you don't know the topic it's very hard to string words together into meaning. Technology, particularly in the form of the cochlear implant, is changing the landscape of deafness rapidly and in amazing ways, yet the fact remains that, given the fluid nature of sound and speech, it's a constant struggle for the hearing-impaired person to connect easily with the hearing world.

While I agree with Helen's observation, I also know deafness has *opened* me to connections with people and other beings that I might not have become aware of had I not lost my hearing. In the everyday world I learned early on that we don't hear with the physical ears alone. The other senses, the eyes particularly, are, whether one is aware of it or not, constantly listening to the world. Lip reading involves far more than watching the lips. The expression in the eyes, the tightness, or ease of the muscles around the mouth, the hand gestures and bodily posture, all can reinforce or contradict the words read on the lips. The lips can say one thing and the eyes another. The effects of words on others can also be read even if one isn't able to catch the words themselves. I remember one time when my parents confronted my brother. I didn't know what the matter was, but he denied being involved in whatever had happened. I saw that my parents believed him. I saw too that he was lying, and he was lying because he was scared.

As the multiple dimensions of human interactions became more transparent I felt myself to be a participant rather than a spectator. In the example just given I connected and sympathized with my brother's anxiety. Whether he'd done wrong or not didn't cross my mind at that young age. He was my adored older brother, I believed wholeheartedly in his goodness, and my only thought was to stand by him.

There were others whom I felt connected to in this way also, though I didn't talk much with them. They gave me the reassurance and contentment that can come through the gift of simply *being with* another. They accepted who I was, as I was, without explanations. In effect they *saw* me. To them I was another human being, not "the handicapped kid." The janitor in my elementary school was one such person, the switchboard lady was another, the farmer who sold us vegetables out of his truck was a third. There was also the dog that appeared on our back steps, and reappeared after a man who claimed the mongrel was his came and took him away. Though we legally adopted him, he really adopted me. Friday, as we called him because he first arrived on a Friday, kept me informed about people through every bodily stance, be it the wag of his tail or the cock of his ears. I was never friendless, never unconnected as a child, even though someone at school left a note on my desk saying, "Deaf girl—go home," and the girl who lived next door to us, who my parents had thought was my best friend, would not have anything to do with me.

There are other things I heard, too. I often heard people's thoughts before they put them into words. I knew when my father was working on a business problem and when my brother was about to come up with a youthful invention, be it a rocket ship or a photographic experiment. This has nothing to do with mind reading. Many thoughts are not manufactured in our brain, as most believe, but come to us from the realm of thought beings and can be detected as they are coming. They are far more than the "intellectual machinations" we ordinarily associate with thinking. Though I was unable to express it until much later, it was evident to me that the thoughts some people harbored were rather dead while others were amazingly alive. In one history class in high school the teacher seemed to be trapped in a box of old musty knickknacks and notions. I found it sad and stifling. The one year of art history I took was an altogether different story. The teacher, an artist herself, approached every painting and every art slide with one thought: can the observer also experience the creative process of this particular work?

"Let's not talk now about whether you like it or not," she'd say. "Look at what's going on here." One day when looking at slides of the interior of Chartres Cathedral it seemed to me I was quite literally looking at a pulsating organism of thoughts. Arches, buttresses, naves, the placement of aisles, altars, pews, stained glass windows, and sculptures all stood by themselves yet breathed together. I sensed too that the thoughts behind these outer forms had not only been created and brought together over many, many years by groups of like-minded people whose aspirations were in amazing accord, they had come from another, higher realm that I could only vaguely sense. The overall effect on me was one of deepest awe.

For me thoughts and feelings were, and always will be, entwined. Speaking of feelings, I could when quite young step into a room full of people and be aware, immediately, that someone there was deeply troubled or depressed. I could find this person within a matter of minutes and would often stand near him or her, not talking, as though physical proximity might bring that person some relief.

I also heard an inner voice. This voice offered me comfort when I was feeling unconnected and very commonsensical suggestions when I was confused. For example, I might hear, "You're okay" when in the midst of a group of peers whose speech I couldn't follow, and I believed it. Or I'd hear, "Go help your mother" when I was feeling sorry for myself, and the words would move me right into action and out of self-pity. I never questioned the voice. I heard it clearly and almost always instantaneously. There was none of the uncertainty or the hassles often associated with ordinary everyday communications. No, "What did you say? Please say it again." I trusted it, acted on it, and assumed everyone had access to a private inner voice. Though I discovered later, when I first described the inner voice to my best friend at age thirteen, that others didn't know what I was talking about, I believe to this day that everybody, no matter what his or her religious upbringing or personal spiritual beliefs, can connect with this source of inner comfort and guidance. Physical deafness is certainly not a requirement for its discovery.

The inner hearing was, and continues to be for me, another dimension to life. While people marvel that I hear inner voices, I marvel at the truly amazing powers of healthy human ears and how the brain works when it comes to everyday hearing, protecting oneself from invasive sounds, sorting through the information that's pouring in, and connecting through speech. Along the same line, I know that this other dimension I've become aware of is certainly not the "all" of what we call the invisible or spiritual world of which every one of us is a member. I know others inwardly see and hear things I can't see or hear. I know that more and more young people today are aware of these dimensions and need our trust in what they are perceiving, and our belief in their integrity and courage. I also know that there is a good deal more I would like to be able to see and hear inwardly, not out of mere curiosity, but out of a longing to serve the inner guide who has befriended me for so long.

It is with this in mind—and heart—that I want to explore the possible implications of an aspect of inner perception I became aware of shortly after I lost my hearing. This is the realm of the dead. In the chapters that follow I will share experiences I've had of friends who were dying and others who have passed over, trusting light will shine on these events as they are remembered. Part One is an assortment of experiences that, for the most part, "happened" to me. Though consciously involved in all of them, I did not actively seek them out. Part Two is about one connection in particular through which I have tried, and am still trying, to attune regularly and consciously to the other half of life.

The dead are all around and are as much our neighbors as the family next door, the tree at the corner, the birds at the feeder. We need not be on speaking terms with all our neighbors, but the recognition of their presence, if only in a form of a nod, a smile, or a thought of appreciation and thanks, can go a long way. When we acknowledge each other we affirm and quicken life in each other. Though we may not be able to see the dead outwardly or inwardly, openness to their presence means a great deal to them, as I hope to illustrate in the pages ahead.

I believe too that we need to venture beyond the common view of death. Death is far more than the external aspects we ordinarily associate with it—someone we know has died and is apparently gone; physical bodies are reduced to ashes, buried in the earth or blown apart; we read of deaths, often in great numbers, daily in the newspaper and hear of them constantly on TV; we know we ourselves will one day die. It's my impression, based on my experiences, both the ones that "happened" and the ones I've asked for in full consciousness, that those on the other side want to share with us the *inner* nature of the external aspects of physical death. They not only wish to enlighten us, they crave our participation in their experiences because our participation can, in turn, help and enlighten them.

The veil between the worlds is becoming thinner. Our inner ear of ears and eye of eyes wait to open, to awaken, in ways we must dare to imagine.

A NOTE TO THE READER

Some names have been changed and others have been omitted in the accounts that follow. This is because I understand, from what I've been told, that a soul is *much* larger than the name he or she carried in one lifetime. And it can be confining, even painful, to be called up by that name.

"We must be filled with a profound awe for everything human, even in our memories and recollections."
— RUDOLF STEINER, *How to Know Higher Worlds*

PART I
FIRST AWAKENINGS

When Children Die

M<small>Y FIRST EXPERIENCE</small> of death occurred when I was in the hospital after I lost my hearing from the mumps. The advent of deafness was very dramatic—one day I could hear, the next I couldn't. I'd just turned six and so, fortunately, was old enough to know what language is all about. (Those born deaf must learn this through long, hard work.) I was also young enough not to be aware of the negative associations attached to words. Words like "deaf," "death," "dead," or "dying."

There was a boy on my floor who was dying. He was extremely thin and his facial coloring was terrible. My guess now is that he had cancer. I'm not sure how we met but I was allowed to visit him a couple of times, sometimes twice a day, and, as he couldn't get up, we pretended the sheets on his bed were mountains, caves, valleys and plains over which my stuffed animals roamed. We didn't talk much, yet we connected easily the way children the world over connect through play. I provided most of the activity, as he was deeply weary and it was an effort for him even to move his arms.

I felt how his health was receding while mine was returning full force. It was very hard for me to sit in a wheelchair as the nurses requested when taking me around the hospital, because I was itching to move. All I knew was that my hearing had been switched off, the doctors were baffled, my parents were worried, the nurses could be cranky, and watching faces was the only way I could understand others. It was not only strange not being able to hear others, it was strange not being able to hear my own voice. For some time I was afraid I'd lost my voice as well as my hearing.

It happened that I suddenly wasn't allowed to visit my friend, and nobody would tell me why. Even if I'd had my hearing I doubt they would have told me the truth. I decided to find out for myself what was going on, put on my bathrobe, slipped down the hall to his room and peeked in. There were more nurses, doctors and machinery in there than I'd ever seen. There was an air of panic, too. Though I couldn't see him because of all the commotion, I knew he was leaving his body, and no one wanted that. But I was relieved. My sole thought, as the nurses caught sight of me and hurried me out and back to my room, was, "Hooray! Now you'll be able to run around like me!"

Hours later I woke in the middle of the night certain he was standing by my bed and was no longer weary. I greeted him and went back to sleep.

❧

Perhaps it would help if I explain here that inner impressions come to me in several ways. In their simplest form they may merely be the very definite feeling that someone is there. If you have ever taken a walk during a really dark night alongside another person and been aware of his or her silent presence moving beside you (forget about being able to hear the footsteps), you will know what I mean when I speak of knowing someone is there, though you cannot see a face or form. You may also sense what's going on in the person: uncertainty when it comes to walking in the dark, preoccupation, delight in the stars, whatever. In a similar way it's possible to sense the general mood of a deceased person whom you can't see.

Another common impression is that of being watched. As an analogy, take the time when I was hiking through the woods, stopped beside a river and, after a few minutes, sensed that someone was looking at me. I looked across the water and into the thicket of many-colored autumn leaves. Gradually I became aware that what I thought was a brown branch was a neck. Then I saw the dark nose, then the watching, waiting eyes. The face of a deer materialized. I was amazed I hadn't seen it right away and was startled and humbled by the realization that it had been there all along. Similarly, you may feel someone is either at a distance or close beside you and is reading your face, or your motions, maybe even hearing your thoughts. Even as I sensed the deer's caution and curiosity that day it's possible to sense the feeling or the intent of the being who is watching you.

Lastly there are impressions that come to me in the form of pictures, like snapshots (both in black and white and in color). They could be compared to dream images that seem to have come out of nowhere and seem to have their own inherent logic and meaning. These pictures, however, come when I'm fully awake and come in a manner similar to the inner voice. I see them within myself even as I hear the voice within myself, and I understand they are conveying something from somewhere else. While I can usually understand what I hear within, inner pictures may need to be interpreted in order to be understood.

ᝈ

To return to the hospital when I was six years old:

The next day, wanting to be sure my friend was indeed free of his sickly physical body, I asked if I could go to his room. The nurses exchanged uncomfortable looks and evaded my questions. I wondered what they were afraid of. I went to his room again when no one was looking and saw an empty bed. That night I again got the impression he was standing beside my bed and was really quite well. This happened twice that night. A few days later I was released from the hospital. In the excitement of going home and returning to school, I forgot about him.

My memory of this experience resurfaced forty-eight years later when I was working on the book *Friend of My Heart*, and my editor asked me to include a chapter about the dead. When it came up I knew it had been there all along, just beneath the surface of my daily consciousness. It was as though my stay in the hospital had occurred the day before, it was that vivid. With it came the impression that my friend, because he hadn't been as deeply embedded in his physical body as an adult is, had passed over quickly. Furthermore I got the impression he had visited me in the years that followed. I have no recollection of these visits. Perhaps I'll remember them after another twenty years. Those on the other side have impressed on me that experiences of this sort, like letters received long ago but not read, can be rediscovered later in life, and only when we are in our physical bodies. If we are out of our bodies we cannot, to continue to speak metaphorically, open and reread the letters. This is a startling reminder of how asleep we must be in our daily waking lives.

Although I was "relieved" at age six that my friend in the hospital was able to leave his body, I have always found it hard to hear of the deaths of children. When I was in my thirties, the six-year-old son of a friend and coworker was killed in an accident. The child and his father were in a clamming boat when a speedboat towing a water-skier went over it. The boy died instantly; the father survived without injuries. The pain of the parents—the mother's hair turned grey within a matter of weeks—was unlike anything I had ever witnessed. When at their home, I got the inner impression that the son, with a bereft expression on his face, was waiting for someone upstairs. I didn't know what to make of this until the mother told me privately that the father refused to go upstairs. Going upstairs meant he would have to pass the door to his son's bedroom in order to get to the master bedroom, and the guilt he felt at having taken his child clamming that day was crushing him. I believed then, and now too, that the child wanted to be "with" his father in the grief and confusion of the sudden separation they were both experiencing. But the father was trapped in guilt and wasn't even able to talk heart-to-heart with his wife about what had happened. For a while it felt as though more than one death had occurred in that family. The marriage, fortunately, survived the tragedy. The parents had counseling separately and together, and some years later another son was born to them.

When I recently came across these words by Rudolf Steiner, the German esotericist and social philosopher whose works have been a source of guidance and help for over forty years, I was reminded of the mournful face of that little boy:

> When little children have died, the pain of those who have remained behind is really a kind of compassion—no matter whether such children were their own or other children whom they loved. Children remain with us and because we have been united with them they convey their pain to our souls; we feel their pain—that they would fain still be here! Their pain is eased when we bear it with them. The child feels in us, shares his feeling with us, and it is good that it should be so; so his pain is ameliorated. (*Life Beyond Death*, p. 235)

I am sure many of you have observed how, in photographs of young children dying from starvation, the faces do not look like the faces of children. They look like old, wizened, sexless beings. I've often thought, "What's going on here?" Once, in response to that thought, an inner impression came to me. I saw discarded seeds—winged maple seeds, acorns, and seeds of the sunflower, marigold, tomato, corn, and zucchini—seeds of all shapes and sizes left on concrete sidewalks and asphalt roads and in dry, dusty ruts. They had apparently been left to wither and disintegrate except that, if I looked carefully, I could see a light pinkish glow, like a thin sheath around them. With the picture came a feeling of wonderment at the number of things that must go right for a single seed to take root, grow, and unfold its potential. Wonderment also at the sheer abundance of possibilities all around, everywhere on this earth, a great many of which are apparently left by the wayside. The light pinkish glow called forth more than wonderment; it called forth joy and deep certainty, certainty that *nothing* endowed with life is lost, or cast away, *nothing is wasted.* What we view as tragedy may be that in name on this physical plane, but in the other realm it may be seen and received as necessary, transforming sacrifice.

Steiner says that the unused life forces of children who die young can and do flow into the lives of those still on earth, both those they were close to and into the larger needs of humanity.

By going into the spiritual world, such souls carry up with them very special forces—forces that would still have been effective here on earth, but that have been prematurely diverted. Those that die early carry with them forces that are especially helpful. (Ibid., p. 38)

I felt a glimmer of understanding of this in January of 2005 when I woke early one morning to the inner picture of an immense bluish-black wave of young faces. Hundreds of small faces, some dark-skinned, some mulatto, others fair. Some were infants, others were closer to puberty. I could not make out their hair color or sex. There was no view of their bodies. All I knew was that they were moving forward as one, almost as if on a roller coaster, and there was an expression that could be seen, like a wash of light pink (similar to the color I'd seen around the seeds) on them. It was an expression of openness, eagerness, and expectancy. I believe I was being given a small glimpse into one aspect of the tsunami of 2004: the forces released over our earth by the deaths of many children all at once.

Although I've received impressions of children who have died, I, myself, have never had the impression the other side is very populated with children. Put this in the form of a question: is growth as we know it in our physical bodies, from birth through childhood, the teenage years, young adulthood, middle age, and on into seniority, mainly a characteristic of life in a physical body on earth? It's my guess that may be the case. I'm certainly *not* saying, however, that we don't experience growth in the afterlife. On the contrary, it seems to me one has plenty to do, but it's another kind of growing than we're familiar with here. Instead of children there are younger and older souls. I'm not comfortable with the terms "advanced" or "less advanced" because we *all*, every one of us, have a role to play in the evolution of the human being. We, in effect, *need* each other in order to grow. Who hasn't met a child one instinctively knows is an "old soul"? Or an adult who seems not only young, but childish or immature?

Why have I received impressions of children on the other side if there aren't many children there? I believe that after death we retain for a while the astral component of the form we were in physically when we died. This is in turn influenced by the fact that we are remembered pictorially in that form by those we were close to who are still alive. Their remembering can hold us in that form, for better or for worse, until we, and they, are ready to move on.

$\mathscr{A}$ STARTLING EXPERIENCE

I DON'T REMEMBER HOW old I was when Mr. Jameson died. I just remember that I roamed the neighborhood a lot on my bike at that time, which means I would have been ten or eleven. Mr. Jameson lived up the hill from us. He and his wife often played tennis with my parents and had two sons who were several years younger than me. One of the boys had a mean streak; I'd seen him throwing stones at a cat, so I always sped up when I went by their house and urged Friday to hurry.

A couple of days after the funeral (which I didn't attend) I thought I saw Mr. Jameson by the back door while I was on my way home. Puzzled, I turned, went partway back up the hill, and coasted slowly by. Both boys were in the yard playing and did not see me—or their father. He was dressed in his outdoor work clothes, which were familiar but strangely colorless. In the last chapter I mentioned inner impressions that are a bit like photographs. It was as if a black-and-white photograph or transparency of him, without edges of any sort, had been inserted over the spot where he stood. He was watching his children with a sad, confused look on his face. I understood his expression had to do with the fact that they were unaware of him.

The next second, Mr. Jameson was gone, or maybe my vision shut down. Only the boys were there, and I wanted to get home.

I was startled and frightened by this experience. There was no denying what I'd seen, and what did it mean? Was Mr. Jameson really dead or had there been some terrible mistake? For some reason I became fixated on the possibility that he'd been buried alive. Even if the logistics of that were beyond me, the possibility was so real that I couldn't bike past their house for a couple of months. If I was in the car and we drove by, I looked the other way.

I'm not sure why I was so frightened but will venture two guesses. First, Mr. Jameson did, in actuality, feel "buried alive," and I was picking up on that. He had died suddenly, unexpectedly, could see and hear his children, probably his young wife too, but they were unaware of him. Second, the worlds were separating for me into "inner" and "outer" and I didn't know what to do about it. I still had no hearing aid, the doctors couldn't recommend one that was powerful enough for me until I was twelve, and I was becoming increasingly aware that, though I heard voices within, I was deaf in the world. Often I would sit through family dinners fully aware I was cut off from the flow of ordinary human conversation. There can be times—I've seen this in my work with deaf children—when those who are hearing-impaired can look as alone as Mr. Jameson looked.

Luckily, despite this experience, I wasn't frightened enough to shut down to the other side entirely. I think it is inevitable that the inner experiences of children are challenged in one way or another as they grow. Mine certainly were. Though I didn't hear anything until later from my parents about their beliefs, I gathered from a friend at school that when you died you went either to heaven if you were good or to hell if you were wicked. She spoke with such authority I didn't dare ask, "What about the back steps of your own house?"

My general feeling was that I couldn't deny what I'd seen. It wasn't a matter of "imagining" I'd seen Mr. Jameson; I *knew* I'd seen him. As no one else talked about seeing anything similar—or maybe I'd missed it because I was deaf—I pushed it all away and down in the back of my memory.

A DEATH IN THE FAMILY

MY MOTHER HAD one sibling, an older brother. He was, like her, very fair, blue-eyed, with a deep laugh and a love of beauty, travel, wild stories, jokes, and liquor. Both were artists. My mother's medium was watercolor; my uncle's was photography. When he came to visit, I swear the temperature in our house went up a couple of degrees because of the energy of their banter.

As a child I got the impression life was hard for my uncle. I suspect he was, like my mother, dyslexic. But they had no name for it back then, and while my mother took hold of all she *could* do and did it with verve, my uncle was pulled down by the feeling he'd been a disappointment to his parents, his father particularly. My uncle's wife was quiet, small-boned, dark-eyed and dark-haired, like a mouse beside a lion. They had no children, and in middle age she became unbalanced. I believe it was Alzheimer's.

When I was thirteen or fourteen my uncle also became ill, and my father took several trips south to help him. Things worsened. I remember my mother talking on the phone with my uncle for hours, and the way she wept after she'd hung up. It seemed to me I could feel darkness coming closer, pressing down, and closing in on all of us. My brother and I tiptoed around. Mealtimes were usually interrupted by more phone calls, not only from my uncle, but also from his doctor or lawyer.

The morning after my uncle died a strange thing happened when my mother told me he was gone. These words popped out of my mouth: "Now you can get on with living."

My mother stared at me, her face paler than I'd ever seen it, and it wasn't just because she wasn't wearing her usual coral lipstick.

"Your uncle just died," she said. "What are you... heartless?"

I could not respond. Her words stung deeply, and I went to school that day wondering if I was in some way responsible for my uncle's death, as if I'd wanted him to die.

When I got home I thought I was going to apologize, but couldn't. The words I'd spoken felt true. To apologize would be canceling out the truth. My mother and I never talked again about this occasion.

I believe those words came from my uncle. He'd fought his battle as long as he could with the demons of disappointment and regret, and now he wanted my mother to get on with her life and to live it *for both of them* with the vitality they'd lived with together as siblings. She did, although understandably it took time for her to travel beyond grief.

It's strange thinking of a person on the other side speaking through one, yet I have, several times, heard those on the other side speak through others and never thought it strange at all. One needs to be able to "hear" the message in the right way or it can be lost or misinterpreted, as I believe happened with my mother and me.

Here's a simple example of an experience, this time as an adult, when I am certain I heard a deceased friend speaking through a living person:

After my friend had died I'd found myself in an unpleasant situation that I thought he was, in ways, responsible for. My basic feeling was, "Well, you got me into this and then you made your exit!" At that time an addition was being built on our house and one morning, after the workers arrived, I discovered my car wouldn't start. The driver's door hadn't shut completely the day before so the interior lights had remained on all night and the battery had gone dead. While I was assessing the situation, one of the workers, a scruffy, balding, pony-tailed guy with a nonchalant air, with whom I'd never exchanged more than a nod or a wave, appeared from behind the house. Without a word he pulled his truck alongside my car and got out his cables. When the car was running again he looked directly at me and said very clearly and distinctly, "Be well." Then he turned and went back to work. Those were the *exact* words my friend often used when we were parting, both in person and when corresponding. My annoyance at the situation evaporated on the spot.

My Grandmother's Journey

Two days before my grandmother died she appeared in a dream to tell me she would soon be on her way. My husband Edward and I were in another part of the country at the time and knew of the cancer but were not sure how close she was to passing over. It's my belief she held on until news reached her of the safe arrival of her first great-grandchild, my brother's daughter. The dream occurred in the early morning of the day my sister-in-law went into labor, though I didn't realize that until later.

In the dream the whole family was gathered for lunch at my parents' house. Everyone, except for me, was sitting on the southern side of the table, facing the northern wall of the dining room. All were talking and, as usual, I was unable to follow the conversation. I was seated facing south and could see beyond the family members opposite me, into the hallway that led into the living room, and then on into the sunroom. The sun was pressing golden-white against the window of that distant room.

My grandmother got up—she'd been seated at the head of the table—and walked into the hallway. No one was aware she'd left. She was in a purple dress and her step was easy. In the living room she turned, looked at me, smiled, and waved. It was not a big, full-hand wave; it was more a little quick twist of the wrist, the kind of gesture a conductor might make. No words were exchanged but love streamed out of my heart toward her. This love, which I felt rather than saw, "touched" a spot on her purple dress above where her heart must have been and she gave a little nod. I felt as though we'd made a pact. Then she turned, walked on into the sunroom, and was gone. My attention was briefly drawn back into the dining room, which looked small and dark. The family was still talking, I was still "out of it," and I woke up.

We did not attend the funeral. Later that month when we went back east for Christmas my mother gave me an oil painting my grandmother had done for me four months earlier of my favorite tree at her home. This, in turn, called forth another dream. In this dream my grandmother was boarding an ocean liner. As she had crossed the Atlantic many times in this manner I was not surprised to see her on the gangplank. Again she smiled, and again I was aware of love streaming toward her.

I was close to this grandmother, but not in the way we think of closeness today: sharing one's ups and downs, speaking often and frankly, doing all sorts of things together. My deafness, and grandchildren in general, made her uncomfortable. She was not active physically; perhaps the most rigorous thing I ever saw her do was clip roses and arrange them in vases. But she did play the piano with great skill and wrote letters in the most beautiful script I've ever seen. She sent me newspaper clippings and books (she loved *The Fellowship of the Ring* and translated it into French) and taught me how to do fine embroidery. The "closeness" had little to do with spoken words and everything to do with beliefs. I knew from the little icons, the books in her bedroom, and some of the sketches in her sketchbook, that she believed in angels and elemental beings. We never discussed these things, but it's because of her—and my grandfather who died when I was eight— that I met certain people who had a huge amount to do with the course of my life and with the development of my own beliefs. She also knew, before I did, that I would marry Edward.

During the six years after my grandmother's death I dreamt of her every six to eight months, and every time she was on a ship. The ship and her situation on it varied a bit, but the thing that really caught my attention was that she was getting younger and younger. I'd always known her on this side as portly—in fact rather shapeless—with tight silver-white curls pressed against her head. She'd used thick, round eyeglasses when reading and sewing, and a cane when walking because of a bad knee. Now here she was becoming more and more slender—really quite shapely—the glasses and the cane were gone, and her hair was turning blonde and growing long.

In the last dream I had of her, the blonde hair was gathered in a swirl atop her head, revealing a delicate neck. She was about eighteen—younger than I was at that time. I would not have known who she was if I hadn't had the earlier dreams and the love they called forth each time. In this dream, for the first time, she spoke to me, and I heard the words without needing to read her lips. She said, "This is how I want to be remembered." I understood as she spoke that the "pact" I'd sensed in the first dream was complete, and we were parting for the time being.

I have no wish to analyze this series of dreams or to speak here of the possible pitfalls of thinking one is communicating with the dead through dreams. There was something truly lyrical about them. They nourished me deeply. Even now when I remember them, like small clear windows into another world, I feel the connecting love, the sense of journey, and the presence of a great, patient ocean all around.

𝒜 True Physician

As a child I knew Dr. Winkler was a significant person because of the way people acted when he was around. Facial expressions can reflect respect as simply and surely as the voice can take on a tone of reverence, and my grandmother and the companion and caretaker who lived with her clearly revered this man. I was specially intrigued by the fact that Dr. Winkler made my gregarious, outgoing mother uncomfortable. Her face would become flushed and her laugh forced. What was it about him, I wondered. He wasn't that imposing physically; he was short, slender, not the least bit overbearing, and had slightly slanted eyes and a thick European accent. He was nearly impossible for me to lip-read, so I couldn't catch what he said. His eyes were watchful, though. I saw that right away.

When I was about thirteen my mother told me Dr. Winkler "knew" all kinds of things about people. She passed on a couple of comments he'd made to her about my brother and me. They didn't register with me at the time. I have the ability, like anybody with normal hearing, to be deaf to what I don't care to hear.

When I was twenty-two my roommate committed suicide and I knew I needed help. Dr. Winkler's watchful eyes and his comments to my mother then came to mind. I wrote him a letter, sent it to him at my grandmother's address, and received his reply within a week. I still have this letter and still marvel at the speed with which he responded. It was as though he did indeed know all about me, even at a distance.

In his letter Dr. Winkler said it is wonderful if one is sensitive, but sensitivity is not helpful, either to the person who exhibits it or to the world, if it is allowed to become hypersensitivity. Sensitivity can weaken or strengthen one, can render one immobile or inspire one to action. Then he raised a question I'd never considered: Why was I deaf? Might there be a meaning to my deafness? He added that when one sense is lost another may open, for behind each physical sense resides a higher sense.

There was no direct mention of my roommate, but his letter brought great solace. Though I didn't write back, I knew there was truth in everything he'd said. I didn't hear the inner voice much at that time, but Dr. Winkler's words had a similar tone of authority, a tone that made me listen. Dr. Winkler also, by way of my grandmother, sent me Rudolf Steiner's *How to Know Higher Worlds.* That, in turn, led to my discovery of Waldorf education and, a short while later, enrollment in a Waldorf teacher training program.

Without conversing with me in person, Dr. Winkler not only challenged me to think in new ways about my life, particularly how I might be of service to others, he also indirectly underlined and affirmed many of the inner experiences I'd had since I'd lost my hearing. After that I was only to see him in person two times before he died. On those occasions I went to him with medical questions, and both times he pointed out the psychological cause behind the physical difficulty. He was always right and knew exactly how much truth I could and couldn't take at a given moment, as though adjusting and administering a dosage of medicine. It grieved me though that it was so hard for me to read his lips because of his accent. I always needed someone to interpret when we were together in person.

Less than a month after Dr. Winkler died, our first child was born, and he came to visit one night after I'd been nursing the baby. Inwardly I saw a full-blown image of him standing beside the cradle looking at our daughter. I'd not been thinking of him and got the impression he was "abroad" checking on various people. I felt him "reading" the baby and was quite eager to know what he saw. His response came to me inwardly and instantaneously—no interpreter needed! The child would be strong-willed and far more active in the outer world of human affairs than I would ever be. That has proven to be true. He also spoke of what he called her "vulnerable or weak spot," making it clear that every such spot in every human being bears within it the potential for powerful personal transformation.

Time went by. I was thoroughly involved in mothering—a second child was born to us—and my writing, and didn't think about Dr. Winkler except when his name came up in conversation. Approximately nineteen years after he'd come to check on our firstborn he returned. I saw no one but knew immediately who it was because of the degree and color of the feelings he always calls up in me. They are awe, respect and fear. Please understand that I mean the word "fear" in a positive, not a negative sense. Dr. Winkler was and is a truth-speaker, and the fear he provokes in me is not fear *of* the truth but fear that I might not be *equal to* it.

By this time I'd been able to live into the questions Dr. Winkler had raised in the letter he wrote after my roommate committed suicide, and I was fully convinced physical deafness has opened, or awoken, me to the presence of higher worlds all around and within. What most people consider a misfortune can be realized as an ongoing opportunity as long as one is determined to "mine" it and find the gold in it, rather than be pulled down by it.

When he returned he had two things to say. I heard his words inwardly as though we were conversing on the telephone. Later, I wrote down all I could remember. First, he said there are individuals on the other side who are intensely interested in what is going on here and hunger to find ways of supporting initiatives with which they are aligned through their soul disposition. These may be ideals to which they devoted their lives while in the body, or they may be ideals to which they have been drawn since passing over. As events are speeding up on earth and these individuals are not yet ready to reincarnate, they need to find ways to connect with their "living contemporaries." (That I believed in reincarnation was assumed in this exchange.) I understood that Dr. Winkler himself—and this came as no surprise—is intent on serving the curative powers inherent in the truth of Christ's second coming. His alignment can best be expressed in these words from the Gospel of St. John: "Ye shall know the truth, and the truth shall make you free" (8:32).

Secondly, Dr. Winkler said it is good if we, on this side, can find ways to help our "dead contemporaries" to see, hear, and experience the truth. Just because they are on the other side doesn't automatically mean they are all-seeing and all-knowing. As David Spangler so humorously and aptly put it, "Death does not confer insight or wisdom like an honorary degree just for losing a body!" Furthermore, said Dr. Winkler, the resistance offered to us by matter, by being in our physical bodies, calls forth great light when we grapple earnestly with questions in search of the truth. This light can help the dead to see.

I did not, I'll admit, know what to make of his comments. What could I do? Where could I begin? And truth—what really did he mean by truth? Finding the hidden meaning in my hearing loss was one thing—and that in itself had taken me years to begin to fathom—this was of another magnitude altogether. I did nothing—or so it seemed at the time. As I look back now I understand that an impulse from a dead mentor or friend can actually enter an individual and begin to work through the person, although in the mind one may think one is doing nothing. The person may think that one must sit down and draw up a great plan, then apply oneself, when the important thing may be simply and faithfully listening and being open. The mind can so quickly shift the focus from the marvel of connecting to one's own personal shortcomings.

Dr. Winkler's words were, fortunately, not completely lost on me. At the time of this conversation I was involved with a group of friends who were meeting every couple of months. Some of the ideas we discussed came from him, though we may not have realized their source. There were also two occasions, months apart, when Dr. Winkler told me to say, "Yes" to someone, and when I did, I was startled both times when tears came into this person's eyes. "Yes" was the answer to a specific question I wasn't even aware had been asked. "Yes" was proof to this person that he was connecting with Dr. Winkler.

Since then I've had sporadic conversations with Dr. Winkler. On one occasion he expressed concern that modern medicine is creating a complex and difficult karma for itself, especially in the delicate matter of prolonging lives through the use of life-support systems. Lest the reader conclude Dr. Winkler was or is disapproving of modern medicine, he has also said that many of these drugs and procedures are "Gifts from the Gods."

Dr. Winkler has often been close when friends and family members have passed over. When I was unable to find or sense the whereabouts of someone I love dearly who had died after an extremely difficult illness, he told

me this person did not want to be found at that time! He
has made it clear we have to respect and honor the path
of every person both on this side and the other. He has
spoken too of the difficulty, for those on the other side,
of exchanging thoughts with the living. As he explained
it, our connection is for the most part achieved through
feeling; not only can we feel what the deceased feel, but
we can also feel and follow their will through impulses
that arise in us. Connecting through thought, on the
other hand, requires *tremendous* energy on their part,
and some are further along than others in their ability to
gather, focus, and impart the energy that accompanies
thoughts. The amount of time one has been on the other
side and the work one is drawn to do there are, apparently, factors in this matter.

I've sensed Dr. Winkler's presence when dealing with
medical situations, both my own and those of family and
friends, and when grappling with difficult children in my
work as a teacher. His visits are not without humor. One
time when I asked for help with a troubled student he told
me to describe the young man in detail. After I'd done so
he said, in effect, "Good job! Now *you* can see the problem—and, if you look, the solution." I've also sensed his
intense interest and joy in the work of certain individuals
who are alive now. Some of these occasions I've found
painful; if only these people could see, hear and connect
with him themselves! If only they realized how very close
their "dead contemporaries" are! Perhaps he wants me to
experience this pain so that I may be spurred on to help
find ways to build bridges between the two worlds.

Dr. Winkler has always known me better than I have
known him, though it seems to me I know him better now,
since he passed over thirty-four years ago, than I ever knew
him when he was on this side. I could share information
with you about his last life on earth, where he was born,

where he worked, his family, all the different walks of life his patients came from (some were quite prominent), how he was a counselor as much as a physician, and so on, but I gather *he* does not want that. For one life is just an eye-blink when viewed from his perspective, and the closest I can come to honoring him in the context of this particular work is to say he has been and continues to be not only a servant of the truth but a *true* physician. The spiritual as well as the physical well-being of every soul he has met are still, even now, a matter of loving interest to him.

This is not a finished chapter, I hope Dr. Winkler will allow me to add more to it with time and as we connect. May I, and others, be equal to the truth and the friendship he offers.

CONNECTIONS MADE
THROUGH THE WRITTEN WORD

BECAUSE OF MY deafness I was a late reader. One might assume reading would come naturally to deaf children, but consider how hard it is to learn to read another language if you don't know or are unsure of the sounds of the words and how they're pronounced. It's common for deaf children to jump over words they can't pronounce when reading, whether aloud or to themselves. The words they can't hear within themselves simply don't exist for them, except as black objects on a page. It's also hard for deaf children to remember how words are pronounced. Even now I, myself, occasionally have a problem with this and have to see a word written phonetically before I can pin it down in memory.

When the written word did open up for me, other worlds opened up as well. That Dr. Doolittle could talk with animals made perfect sense. I read some of his adventures aloud to our dog Friday! When reading I could hear everybody in a story easily, much more easily than in person. My father, who loves great literature, kept handing me books to read: Charles Dickens, Joseph Conrad, Shakespeare, and lesser-known authors like Kenneth Roberts and A. J. Cronin, whom I specially loved. Also, on my own, I discovered Dostoyevsky, Tolstoy, Thomas Mann, Herman Hesse, and the poets. Emily Dickinson,

Robert Frost, Edna St. Vincent Millay, and Dylan Thomas inspired me to try writing verse. Then, in college, I met John Keats, and not only on paper but as a presence.

First, I want to explain that there's a very subtle connection for me between reading and inner hearing. Even as every writer has a different voice—and there's a big difference between the voices of say, Emily Dickinson and Dylan Thomas—every being on the other side, be it a deceased person or an angel, has its own voice. With the written word, a person's handwriting or typing habits, choice of words, phrasing, use of grammar and use of space are all, for me, akin to the visual clues that I pick up when reading lips. When I hear a voice within, there's a similar factor that impresses itself on me, so I often sense immediately (though not always) who is speaking. Since I'm not good at describing tone of voice and things like that, what exactly is this other factor? I call it the *essence* of the being.

I can describe the essence of a voice heard within, or of a presence sensed but not seen, in single words or as colors or as a gesture, sometimes all three. For example, the word that always comes to me when I sense one dear friend, a woman who died a few years ago, is *yearning*. Her color is either sapphire or peach, and I usually sense her standing beside me on the right, close to my ear or cheek, hardly ever in front of me. The word for Dr. Winkler, whom I wrote about in the last chapter, is *servant* or *service*. The word is felt as a noun when he is simply present and observing. When he has something to convey or seems to expect something of me, this word is experienced as a verb. The accompanying color is usually verdant green, sometimes a pale golden yellow. The essence is what enables me to identify the being. Even before a dead person has spoken or tried to make his presence known, his essence may be detected.

Though your experience of a living person, a writer, or a deceased person will quite naturally not be exactly the same as mine, and may well include other dimensions (such as sound), we would probably be more or less in agreement on the essence of that being. And your own essence, like mine and anybody else's, responds differently (with empathy, apathy, interest, aversion, and so on) to that essence. All of this can be said to apply to other aspects of life also: to actors, artists, scientists, birds, animals, flowers, trees, landscapes, and much more.

To return—finally—to John Keats!

I had not thought about any of this when I came across the poetry of John Keats. I only knew that I had to read *all* of his work. I was twenty-one and was like a hound zeroing in on a scent. It grew stronger and stronger as I went from the poems to his letters. Suddenly I was crying as I read what he had to say about the imagination, happiness, Negative Capability, axioms, chambers of thought, the "burden of the Mystery," and "the vale of Soul Making." This isn't the place to describe or discuss those thoughts, and I can't say I really "thought" in any profound way about them at that age. It's that everything in me was saying, "Yes, yes, yes!" to what he wrote *and* to his essence. For—presumptuous as this may sound—I sensed that he was right there. If I'd picked a word then to describe his essence it might have been "spirited." His youth, the death of his love, Franny, his own early death from TB, all these made his situation extremely poignant, and I loved a good romance. But it was the speed and grace with which he advanced from insight to insight that really took my breath away. The last two lines of his last letter, "*I always made an awkward bow. God bless you!*" were accompanied by the inner impression of a smile, warm, bright, and teasing all at once.

Anyone familiar with Helen Keller's life story will remember the moment when Annie Sullivan enabled Helen to make the connection between the cold water gushing into her hands from the pump and the word "water." John Keats was my Annie Sullivan at a certain stage in my life. It was as though he took my hand, placed it over my heart area and said, "*Here* is the soul." And I mean in this instance not only my own soul, but "The Soul" in a universal sense. We awaken in mysterious ways, and though we may think otherwise, we seldom awaken on our own. Even in the course of our busy everyday lives the dead are close by, waiting, hoping to enlarge the boundaries of our wonder.

It's possible I was in love with the idea of John Keats and conjured him up in my imagination. After all, I hadn't yet met a man my age with whom I could talk about poetry, let alone the soul. Yet I sensed his presence not only in the library or when reading outside under a favorite tree; I sensed it when among others. Sometimes I got the impression Keats was pointing, and I found myself looking everywhere at foreheads trying to see what I called "the star." This, quite literally, kept me going during some lonely social times. While others drank beer and experimented with drugs, I looked, peered, and trusted I would someday find those who vibrated to the same thoughts expressed by Keats.

In the spring of my senior year, when coming out of a class one morning, I heard Keats exclaim something that sounded like, "Whoa!" I stopped and stared at a bulletin board covered with announcements of fellowships and summer programs. My attention was drawn to the one right in front of me—there were at least thirty up on that board— for a program at Oxford in England. I knew, without even reading the fine print that I wanted more than anything to go. And go I did. That was where I met Edward.

The letters of Keats were so alive to me that I could *hear* him articulating the words as I read. I've also experienced this when reading the Bible, when reading certain writers, such as Rainer Maria Rilke, and when reading Rudolf Steiner. It's as though words, when they're used in certain ways, by certain souls, become more than symbols that name, show, or explain this or that. They become living powers, streams of inspiration, comfort, and healing, that can flow into the reader many times regardless of when they were written or how many times they are read.

I'm mentioning this because I've often been asked by those on the other side to read specific things. I've been directed to books in libraries and bookstores and have, seemingly out of the blue, received books from people here that souls over there wanted to hear. I've even been told the names or numbers of the chapters I'm to look up, as though being guided to hidden treasure.

Rudolf Steiner speaks in several lectures of the importance of reading to the dead. Here are his words from a lecture given in 1913:

> If human beings on earth allow spiritual thoughts to permeate their souls, those thoughts can be perceived by souls in the beyond, and those earthly souls remain real for them. What we are touching upon here is the fact that the spiritual thoughts nurtured by souls here on earth can not only be perceived but be understood by the souls beyond. And, even more significantly, this fact can have a practical consequence. Building on this insight, we can do something that could become very significant for the relationship between souls here and souls beyond. I refer to what we may call "reading to the dead." Reading to the dead is often extraordinarily important. (*Staying Connected*, p. 30)

Now I will share with you an occasion when I was asked by a friend on the other side to read.

It was early morning, and no sooner had I sat down for my quiet time than I heard, "Psalm 19." I guessed it was a request from my friend John because John told me years ago, long before he died, that number 19 is his favorite psalm. I sensed he'd been waiting for some time for this.

When I'd finished reading Psalm 19, I heard, "Again."

Then, after the second reading, "Again."

By now I was wondering if I was reading the psalm wrong, maybe too fast, not clearly enough, or without real feeling. John had, when alive, often spoken of the importance of knowing how to read aloud so sound and meaning are woven together. He could drive you nuts the way he'd ask you to read something over and over. However, I got the inner impression in response to my hesitation that my reading was fine; he was simply delving more deeply into the psalm each time I read it.

After the third reading I understood that he wanted to hear the Lord's Prayer. It came out very, very slowly. I have never said the Lord's Prayer so slowly. Each line hovered and shimmered in the air. The beauty of it brought tears to my eyes.

When I'd finished there was a long pause, followed by, "Now, *that* was a meal!"

$\mathscr{B}$ARBARA AND TIM

BARBARA WORKED AT the health food store around the corner from where we lived and was in her late forties at the time of this story. When I first met her I couldn't help but notice how much younger she looked at a distance than up close. At a distance you saw her curly · brown hair, trim figure, smart way of dressing, and perpetual tan. Up close you saw two deep lines that looked as though they'd been carved out of her face, beginning at the top of her nose and curving up between her eyebrows into her forehead. The dark rims of her eyeglasses accentuated the lines in an unflattering way, giving her a scarred, wounded look.

Barbara told me her life story bit by bit depending on her mood and the number of customers in the store when I shopped there. She'd gone through an ugly divorce and was still quarreling with her ex, who she claimed was trying to turn their children against her. Her own childhood and teenage years hadn't been smooth. It seemed appropriate that she worked at a health food store—as though such a place might help her find emotional health and balance.

One day in the spring she greeted me with a radiant smile. I discovered the cause of the smile as I was checking out. She'd met "a wonderful guy" named Tim and had fallen head over heels in love. The store became warmer and brighter because of her happiness. I had to laugh when her boss, a poker-faced, buttoned-up type, marveled aloud at how well the business was doing.

Barbara and Tim got married—it was quite possibly the speediest courtship I'd ever heard of. I saw Tim only once when he was coming in the store and I was on my way out. I never actually met or talked with him. He was a large man with a sweet smile and was the manager of a construction company.

Edward and I and the children went away for a month that summer, and I didn't go to the health food store until a couple of weeks after we'd returned. As I came in I sensed something wasn't right. Barbara was ashen. Her first words were, "My husband has to have heart surgery."

Barbara told me Tim had warned her when he proposed that he had a heart problem, but she wanted to get married no matter what happened. Now things *were* happening, and quite a bit sooner than either of them had expected.

Three or four mornings after I'd talked with her I was woken by the impression of a stranger standing at the foot of our bed. I waited and the impression grew clearer. It was a man who was respectfully hoping I'd deliver a message to someone. There were a number of details about his life and words that amounted to this: "She found me when I was lost. She was the light at the end of the tunnel." I wondered what this was all about. When the person (whom I could not see, as there was no accompanying photographic image or anything) repeated the last part about the light at the end of the tunnel, I remembered Barbara, and it "clicked" in me that maybe Tim was speaking.

A few hours later I learned that Tim had died during surgery the day before. I was convinced he was the early morning visitor and was eager to pass the words I'd heard on to Barbara. Just before I entered the funeral home where the wake was being held I again sensed Tim's presence. He asked me *not* to look at the body in the open casket. The implication was that the sadness the viewers emanated as they wept and looked at it exerted a powerful pull on him, and he did not want to be identified with "that powdered thing." (Later it occurred to me that Tim had detached remarkably quickly from his physical body, especially considering the fact that the death had been sudden. Perhaps he'd had a near-death experience earlier in his life and knew what to expect. I never got to ask Barbara about that.)

Barbara was with her children in an adjoining room. She didn't want to be near the casket and, to my surprise, looked a lot better than the last time I'd seen her. When I told her what I'd heard from the early morning visitor her face lit up. Every detail I'd heard about Tim's life was correct, and there was no way I could have learned these intimate things except from Tim himself or from Barbara, and she knew she'd never spoken of them to anyone. Then I passed on Tim's message, which was really a message of profound thanks that they had met and had time together and how she had been the light at the end of his tunnel.

It's an amazing experience when you know you've helped love to find its way between two people. Barbara did not doubt for a minute that everything I'd told her was coming from Tim. She thanked me profusely, and I, I'll admit, went home feeling rather pleased with myself.

Then things got sticky.

Barbara, quite understandably, was desperate to talk with Tim through me. I was able to connect with him again and to pass more words on to her, but a feeling of acute discomfort grew and grew in me. When Barbara gave me a gold bracelet as a token of thanks I could not accept it, nor could I explain why I couldn't accept it.

There were other gifts she wanted to give as well as offers of cash, but I beat a hasty retreat. I shut both the outer and inner doors on her and Tim.

Why did I do this?

The whole thing not only made me uncomfortable, it scared me. I was happy to pass on a message of thanks but terrified at the prospect of being asked to get answers to personal questions. I also found the thought of payment downright repugnant.

Now, over twenty-five years later, I'm glad I shut the door at that time, in that situation. I did not know a thing about life after death or the dangers of getting caught up in the glamour of being a medium. I can't say I know a lot more now, and I don't want to give the impression I'm condemning people who are known as mediums or spiritualists, for I've had hardly any experience of them. I firmly believe that any situation in which one has power over another, or others, because one is able to see or hear into the higher worlds *must* be overseen by Christ if it is to be a blessing to all.

To explain more fully what I mean:

I'm a Christian but I do not belong to any religious denomination. I believe Christ is here now and is available to all of us as comforter, guide, and friend, whether or not we know of or believe in him. This means there are people who meet him who may not know who he is, but may realize they are in the presence of someone or something extraordinary. (Quite a few who have had a near death experience speak of meeting, as they passed over, a being of light who is, in my opinion, the Christ. If interested in such accounts, see the list of suggested readings at the end of this book.) What is spoken of in Biblical terms as the Second Coming is, in my opinion, occurring *right now*. Christ has come again, but not in a physical body such as we associated him with when he came as Jesus Christ. He is in an etheric body, and cannot be seen in the ordinary way through the physical eyes. He is here to enable both us, the living, and the dead to become all we are capable of becoming.

To attempt to fit these beliefs into the context of what I was saying about Tim and Barbara, and why I felt queasy about taking on the role of medium with them:

I believe Christ sees me, the situations in which I find myself, and those I come into connection with, a million times more clearly and profoundly than I myself am able to see them. He knows I may judge a situation wrongly. He knows that even if I want to be of help, my efforts may prove to be meddlesome. I intuitively sensed I was not equal to what Barbara was asking of me. And it may be Barbara and Tim were also, back then, not equal to what Barbara wanted.

I've arrived at a point in my life where I know my good intentions are important and can in themselves be a form of blessing to others, but they're not enough. To be truly helpful I need knowledge, *His* knowledge. I can ask, and we are all encouraged, indeed *urged*, to ask for help in this matter of being of help between the living and the so-called dead. At the same time, nothing can be forced. The help Christ offers comes through love, and love cannot be cajoled, pinned down, organized or manufactured in the way of ordinary human thinking. It must be allowed to move and unfold out of its own will, in its own time.

$\mathcal{S}$UICIDE

IN AN EARLIER chapter I mentioned the suicide of a roommate. Here is what happened:

When I was twenty-two I shared a room at the International House in New Haven, Connecticut with a lovely Czechoslovakian girl named Yula. She was a chemist at Yale and I, a would-be poet, was working in the University biology department. During the course of the four months we roomed together I saw her step back from life, slowly at first, as though needing a few extra hours of sleep, and then more and more rapidly until she was unable to get up at all in the morning to go to work and would spend almost the entire day in bed facing the wall.

Early on I knew something was wrong and talked more than once with the overseers of the House. They said they had known Yula longer than I, that she had been depressed in the past, and had come out of it before. There were days when I felt Yula was screaming for help but everyone in the house was deaf and getting deafer. I tried to engage her, suggested we double date with some guys I knew, brought her special foods, and invited her to stay with my family at Christmas. She just shook her head and smiled her wan smile.

The morning of the day I went home for Christmas vacation I blew up. Yula was, as usual, facing the wall. I told her she had to think about something other than herself, that she had to get out or she'd be sucked up altogether. She didn't respond. So I said with all the force I could muster, "Stop being so selfish!" She turned to look at me and I thought I'd finally reached her. She said she needed to rest during the holidays, thanked me for the invitation, and added that she wanted to give me her palm plant. She knew I loved plants. She knew too that I'd been taking care of the scrawny thing all along. I was touched that she was giving it to me and only later realized she had, at that moment, finalized her own plans. The next day she died of a drug overdose.

I not only struggled with the feelings of helplessness her suicide called up in me and wrote Dr. Winkler as described in an earlier chapter, there were moments when I knew very well that the force that had led her to take her own life was also present in me. It's my guess that many of us contemplate suicide at one point or another. We may do it because the loneliness is too great, the disappointment with our lot is too pervasive, or the feeling of despair over the condition of *everything* in the world is more than we can bear. Like Yula we may just want to curl up and go to sleep.

We may also play with the idea of suicide because we may want, unconsciously perhaps, to tease or test others: our parents, the boyfriend who unexpectedly said, "It's over," the boss who never understood us, even God.

"Look God, here's this knife in my hand," the suicidal person might say. "If I don't hear from you in the next ten minutes I'm going to plunge it into my heart."

When nothing happens, the person changes the rules a bit and the game continues until it all seems silly, one is distracted, or the knife winds up in the heart.

I'm no expert on the topic of suicide. I know it is a delicate and complex subject, but this book would be incomplete if I didn't mention it. When I remember Yula now what comes back to me is the frightening feeling of her being "sucked up." Those were the words I used when addressing her. *What* was sucking her up?

I believe it's possible to sense the general flow of the life force when with a living person. It can be evident, even to a casual observer, whether a person's vital energy is moving outward, resting, stagnating, fading, or receding, in the same way that it can be evident whether a plant or an animal is thriving or not. This is quite apart from whether a person is, in personality, coming on strong or weak, and whether that person appears to be confident or unsure. It is also quite apart from the age of the person, although the vital energy certainly moves differently in different stages of life. The energy of a teenager can really be popping compared to that of an elderly person!

It is normal for the vital energy to flow in and out, even as day flows into night, and night flows out again as day. Or as summer flows into autumn, autumn into winter, and winter out again into spring and on into summer. But with Yula I didn't sense any balance between the in and out. It was all backward, inward, downward, slowly when I first met her, then faster and faster. The thing that was sucking her up had, for me, a color and a sound. It was a dark muddy green and gave off a droning sound. I don't remember what I was thinking when I told her to stop being so selfish (those words haunted me later, I worried I'd pushed her over the edge) but I know it was an attempt to stop the backward, inward movement. There are times when I feel that pausing for a minute, just one minute, to let in the *right here and now*, which is God, can save anyone from anything. But Yula couldn't pause.

After she died the Czechoslovakian embassy came in to pack up Yula's belongings and send them to her parents. I learned quite a few things about her. Foremost among them was her very great love for her country and her despair that it would ever be free of the Communist regime (this was in the 1960s). I learned this from a therapist the embassy had helped her find. I hadn't been aware she was having therapy, nor was I aware of her political disaffection, or the fact that she was homesick and, at the same time, terrified at the prospect of going home. Her departure from the US would have been the following spring. I believe she was sucked up by despair, both personal and national. It was my first exposure to the reality of the deep ties a person can have with her homeland. That a person's very life force could be entwined with the life force of a country was a new concept to me.

I had little to no sense of Yula's presence after she died. I was probably too caught up in my own emotional reaction to be open to her. At the same time, it was a great shock to discover that I'd been sharing space with a person about whom I'd really known *nothing.* Suddenly I was determined to be of help to other people—who or how wasn't clear—and left my job and the International House. I took the palm plant she had given me, and to my amazement it shot up, filled out, and flourished. When I married Edward a second palm head sprouted off the central trunk. Two more palm heads followed four and six years later, after the births of our daughters! Quite apart from the pleasure of a handsome plant, Yula forced me to turn a corner in my own life, as was evidenced in my departure from that area and my exchanges with Dr. Winkler. I trust she feels the depth and warmth of my gratitude.

❧

Seen in the light of her love for her country, there's almost a quality of glamour to Yula's suicide. Sometimes when I read of suicide bombings I remember her. The other suicides I now remember have not been glamourous at all.

There was my brother's girlfriend who jumped from a city window. The cause was never clear, though Debby's parents very thoughtfully made sure my brother knew Debby had *not* been hiding an unwanted pregnancy. I only knew Debby from a distance. When I spent time with my brother right after her death, I was aghast at the feeling of pointlessness that accompanied him. I believe Debby jumped because she felt there was no meaning to life and, on the other side, found herself in the same dark prison. I prayed earnestly that my brother would recover from the loss and not be affected by her malaise. He did recover. He's a man of high purpose.

There was the wife of one of the teachers at the school where my husband taught. I can't remember how she took her life and don't feel the need to remember. What I do remember is that she was a tall, quiet woman with four children who were often a handful. Her husband's eyes were dark, deep brown while hers were light blue and very wistful. At the service I felt she craved music, grand lofty music, and felt she had gone over in a condition of deep weariness and discouragement. A mood of apology settled on the room, as though she was saying, "I'm *so* sorry. I'm *so* tired, I just couldn't go on." It seemed to me that the best thing we could do for her would be to offer music, live or recorded, and allow her to immerse herself in that without any reminder of our sadness or disappointment. I'm sure there is some wisdom at work in the fact that one of her children became the business manager of an internationally known and acclaimed dance company.

There was the son of a colleague at work who hung himself. He was in his late twenties. Nothing seemed to be going the way he wanted, and the picture that came across of him was of one quite aimless, even bored. His mother, a generous spirit and an extremely hard worker, was stunned by the death. When we went to the funeral home to offer our sympathy and support we found it jammed. We were waiting in line to have a word with his mother when a vivid inner impression of him came through. He was standing near us looking this way and that like a dazed man wandering about in a train station. "All these people are here to see my mother," I heard him say. "They don't know me, they don't know me at all; they're here for her." He was right. He'd thrown away a chance to make real connections such as you can only make on earth. I felt pity for him. As he didn't seem, even then, to want to connect, I did not address him.

The inner impression I received from this last suicide and from certain other similar situations was that the unhappy soul discovered nothing had changed, he could not escape himself, he found himself in the same place that drove him to take his life. I've thought and prayed about suicide and believe, as of this writing, that there's a paradox embedded in it. On the one hand, we are free, absolutely free, to do whatever we want with our life. Life is the ultimate gift, and God has given us the power to choose what we want to do with this gift. If we choose to throw it away, that's our business, and we'll have to deal with the consequences. On the other hand, our life is not truly ours until it is given in service to God.

Lastly I'd like to speak of a beloved friend who struggled mightily with the fact that four members of her family had committed suicide over the course of many years. She told me that she and one of her surviving sisters had made an agreement as young women that they would die natural deaths. Both did. There were times, though, when my friend seemed to be in the grip of demonic forces. The spells were characterized by rage, near hysteria, an inability to listen or to focus on anything anyone was saying, and certain self-destructive gestures (which, fortunately never went beyond being gestures). When I first witnessed one of these spells a powerful certainty came to me: I should not pay attention to the negative things I was seeing with my eyes, I should, rather, direct my inner eye on the good, beautiful, true soul I knew and loved. This doesn't mean I didn't try, in simple ways, to restrain her. I did. But basically, I looked for and addressed the best in her, and it always reemerged. Later she would say, "I don't know what happened" or "What came over me?" and would be apologetic, if not ashamed. Nevertheless, the good prevailed. I have seen similar behavior in a few of my students over the years and have tried also with them to seek out and appeal to their best selves. It always helps. Holding to the highest, most truly human recollections we may have of those who have passed over—whatever their path to the other side—is, I am certain, also of help to them.

ANNABELLE

ANNABELLE WORKED AS a maid for my grandmother. When my grandmother died Annabelle came to help my mother, occasionally at first, and then for longer and longer periods. She was tiny Irish woman with forget-me-not blue eyes and a large head of white hair that always made me think of a dandelion in its final stage before the seeds are scattered every which way. After our second child was born Annabelle came to us daily for a week to help keep the house clean. Her particular enthusiasm was the garbage. No sooner had I put a Kleenex tissue in the wastebasket or a dirty diaper in the pail than it was whisked away and disposed of or washed out.

Though she had one daughter and, I believe, some grandchildren, Annabelle had no husband and was a very solitary person. Her solitude and her role as a servant seemed to have whittled her right down to her spare bony frame. Though my mother would offer her a cocktail at cocktail time (which she frequently took) and meals with us, it always seemed to me that Annabelle was most comfortable reading the newspaper and tabloids alone in her room or eating bread by herself at the kitchen table. I can't remember her in anything other than her tidy white uniform and blue cardigan sweater, nor can I remember conversations with her, except for the last one we had together.

It was Easter Sunday sometime in the 1980s when my mother and I suddenly turned to each other in the middle of lunch and asked the exact same question: "How is Annabelle?"

At the time, Annabelle had not been working for my mother for some months, and, because her daughter with whom she was residing lived closer to us than to my mother, it was natural that my mother asked me. At the same time, my mother was the one for whom Annabelle worked, not us, so my asking her made the most sense.

Neither of us knew how she was and both of us felt strangely concerned. My mother went out to the kitchen and dialed Annabelle's number but got no response, so I said I'd go by her daughter's house the next day.

"Get her some flowers," said my mother.

"And French bread," I added because that was Annabelle's favorite food.

The next morning the local flower stores were closed and all I could find was a leftover lily plant at the supermarket. I took that and the French bread, went to the daughter's house, and rang the front bell.

There was no response. There was no car in the driveway, and no neighbors were at home, yet I *knew*—don't ask me how—that she was in the house. So I went to the back door, which was locked like the front door yet had a view of the hallway inside, and pounded on it. Five minutes went by and I pounded again.

Then, like a sleepwalker, Annabelle appeared. She walked right through the hallway into another room and out of sight. Again I pounded, and when she reappeared she came to the back door. She was in a partially fastened nightgown—it was a shock not to see her in her neatly buttoned uniform. Her hair was disheveled and her eyes were quite unfocused. She unlocked the door, and when I stepped into the house she walked right into my arms.

After all the brief kisses on the cheek she'd allowed me to give her over the years, her greeting was rather unsettling. When she finally stepped back she seemed to have remembered who she was as she fastened her night-gown, fetched her bathrobe, and asked if I wanted a cup of coffee. I said no thanks, but we sat down and talked. I learned that her daughter and her family were away and had left enough food for Annabelle for about a week and a half. She seemed happy to get French bread, as they'd bought an Italian brand, but she said she wasn't hungry. Nor was she aware that Easter had come and gone. Then she asked what month it was, what day, and what time.

I was troubled by her disorientation, not to mention her being left all alone (she was then in her eighties) and suggested she come to our house. Annabelle did not want that, and repeatedly said she'd be fine. When I got up to leave I promised to return the next day. She said that wouldn't be necessary. I finally got her to agree I would come two days later in the afternoon with another loaf of French bread and the newspaper. She thanked me, saw me to the back door, allowed me to give her a kiss on each cheek, and waved good-bye from the window.

On some level I knew I would never see her again. I knew we were really saying goodbye and she wanted to die alone, by herself. But first she needed to be reassured she was remembered, thought about, loved. Later, when I worked in hospice as a volunteer I heard many stories of people who wished to die by themselves, yet needed a push or a "sign" that it was okay to leave.

Annabelle's daughter returned the next afternoon. She found her mother on the living room floor beside the lily in her nightgown and robe, as though she'd lain down to take a nap. I did not connect again with Annabelle after that Easter Monday. It may be she wants to be as solitary and quiet on the other side as she was when here.

$\mathcal{T}$HE FIRE OF CANCER

WHEN I WAS thirty-five, the father of four remarkable young people who were or had been students at the school where Ed taught, came down with cancer of the lungs. Though this family, like every family, had its points of tension, it was a very close-knit and extremely hardworking family. Mike, the father, was a philosophy professor at a nearby university. The mother, Leah, who was European by birth, had a menial job. Leah's main work was her family and taking care of herself, as she'd had looming health problems when her children were younger. They lived simply in a tiny house by the Atlantic Ocean, in a community that quadrupled in size during the summer and shrank dramatically during the cold, windy fall and winter months. As I remember they had one car, a delightful old tub, and had sacrificed many of the comforts and conveniences most of us take for granted today in order to give their children the best possible education. I felt it to be an unspoken given in that household that all the children would aim high, do as well as they could, and contribute toward the good of the world. Moreover, they *did* do amazingly well and, I'm sure, are still shining and leading the way in their respective fields.

That Mike had cancer was a concern for everyone at the school, not only because he was the main breadwinner, but also because of Leah's past health history. The eldest child, a noble fellow who shared his father's name, had visited us at our cabin in New Hampshire one summer while on a bicycle trip. After that I always looked for him at school events and rejoiced when he was accepted at an outstanding college, and later at medical school. It was because of this friendship that I found myself reaching out to the parents, first with a note of good will, then with weekly casseroles, and eventually—as I was as strongly drawn to them as to their eldest—with all the care, respect, and love I could offer. The six months of Mike's last year on earth were, for me, a crash course in the art of simply being "with" a struggling, suffering human being, in the same way that others had simply been "with" me when I was a confused, struggling deaf kid.

When I first visited school had just started, Leah's tomato plants were groaning beneath the weight of over-ripe fruit, clouds of monarch butterflies were beginning their journey south, and death was far from our thoughts as Mike and I sat on their sun-drenched deck getting to know one another. During the next three months glorious, bright, wild hope was always present when I visited. I say "glorious, bright, wild hope" because Mike had had cancer before and everyone knew the odds were stacked against him. But that was never mentioned. There was *always* the chance fate could be outwitted, grace would descend, a miracle would occur.

I became the class—never mind if it was a class of one—that Mike was unable to teach. In the beginning he talked about philosophy, history, and politics. Then, as the temperature dropped outside and the effects of chemotherapy began to take their toll, we were forced inside, both literally and metaphorically, and the conversation became more personal. I remember being startled when I arrived one day to find him in bed, no longer in his easy chair or at the kitchen table. Mike was a tall, handsome man. I've always thought of him as a Viking in both color and temperament. It was strange going from looking up, or across and into, his dark blue eyes to looking down into them. The image of a great stag being forced to its knees came to me more than once as he traveled from a vertical to a horizontal state of being.

Mike adored his children and talked about them more and more as the thoughts he'd worked with as a professor began to seem cumbersome and fell away one by one. At first Mike asked about our children, and then he roamed over the topic of parenthood, sharing memories from his own childhood as he went. He had two sons and two daughters, evenly spaced: first a boy, then a girl, then the second son, and the second daughter, in that order. I know there were others who thought he expected too much of his children, was frankly over-involved in their lives, but I didn't feel I could or should judge anything in that configuration.

After Christmas when it was evident that hope had gone from being glorious, bright, and wild, to being small, muted, and threadbare, the second son took a semester off from college so somebody would always be at home with Mike. I marveled not only at the quality of teamwork in this family; I marveled that it was Patrick who chose to be there. Patrick was the one Mike was most concerned about at that time. He was also the one who most resembled his father. I have to laugh when remembering one heated conversation between the two. What the topic was doesn't matter.

"The thing is...." Mike argued, wagging his right index finger at his son.

Ten minutes later, Patrick quite unconsciously began a sentence with a similar wag of the same finger and the words, "But the thing is, Dad..."

I'm trying to present Mike's path toward death as fully as I can, despite the passage of many years between then and now, not just because it's a moving story, but because it was evident that all in that family, not just Mike, were going through many small deaths month by month, as well as day by day. These deaths not only represented the deaths of personal dreams (such as losing a husband one hoped to grow old with), they were also examples of sacrifice (such as Patrick giving up a semester at college). It was as though the cancer was not only burning up Mike's physical body, it was burning away all that was unnecessary and all that stood in the way of intimacy in that already frugal and close family. Each member of that family was becoming more beautiful, every greeting you exchanged with every one of them was becoming more poignant, every conversation came quickly to the point, even when gallows humor emerged. Tears came easily, laughter too. Often when I drove home after visiting Mike—there were emergency hospital visits also—I felt as though I'd been sitting beside a fire and my face and body remained warm for days afterward. I felt deeply privileged to be a part, not only of their family at that time, but of the family of humanity. For the approach of death made life indescribably, almost unbearably, real, vivid, and precious.

It is widely known that when we die we go through a life review. Mike went through much of that before passing over. As he shared experiences, mused over them, struggled with aspects of them, and let them drop away, his body began to glow. I suppose drastic weight and hair loss had something to do with this, but to my eyes he never looked humanly diminished. A white light pulsated gently within. When the cancer spread into his brain, taking away the use of his eyes, speech organs, and thinking, my attention was drawn to his hands. It was as though what was left of his consciousness had retreated to his fingers. If anyone knows what I mean when I say a hand can be articulate, and I'm speaking here of touch rather than gesture, they will know what I mean when I say his hands became his voice. I sat by his bed and held either one or both of his hands. They told me again and again how much he loved his wife and his children. One by one he named and blessed them. He could not bring himself to let go of them, and because of this, his last weeks were drawn out and difficult.

Mike's family knew the end was near and were determined to nurse him at home. Three days before he passed over I saw him in a vivid dream. He was towing their sailboat out to the harbor. I couldn't see who was driving the old tub, but there was Mike in the boat, upright, hale, hearty, ready to go. After two days, when the phone call announcing his death didn't come, I drove out to see what was going on.

Patrick, guitar strung over one shoulder, greeted me at the back door. He looked fried.

"What's the matter?"

"I'm *so* tired," he admitted. "Why can't he just go? We'll be fine.... I know we'll be fine."

"Why don't you tell him?"

We went into the bedroom. Mike was lying on his back, eyes closed, mouth open, motionless, except for the slow rise and fall of his chest. It was late afternoon and rather dark. We each took one of his hands. Patrick told his father whatever he needed to tell him, after which we said the Lord's Prayer, and tiptoed out.

The next morning, when Patrick was strumming his guitar in the kitchen, he stopped, suddenly realizing silence had descended in the adjoining room. And what a silence! He said it almost made his hair stand on end. His father had stepped over.

The funeral was well attended and very heartfelt. Mike seemed flattered by the turnout, moved by the words of the priest, and impatient with the casket, as though the money that had gone for that and the funeral home could have been used for more important things. Though I could not see him, I felt him standing behind Leah almost the entire time as though shielding her from a draft.

It was my impression that Mike's formal entry into the afterlife did not actually occur until about six months later. Still unable to let go of his loved ones, he remained close. Whenever I saw them, singly or as a family, he was there: a taciturn, almost heavy presence. I had two or three dreams in which he appeared. In one he was trying to let Patrick know that the deep sea diving equipment Patrick was trying out wasn't hooked up properly. It seemed to me that the equipment had to do with higher education (both college and graduate school). I could see in the dream that Patrick wasn't in any danger, though Mike might have thought so. I woke with the understanding that over-protectiveness of one's children can sound to them like doubt, even mistrust of their abilities and judgment. I shared the dream with Patrick, but first told Mike as simply as I could what the dream had revealed to me.

"Don't you trust Patrick?" I asked.

There was no response.

"He is the spitting image of *you*! Don't you trust yourself?"

An impression of waves of tender warmth, bearing thanks, came to me.

෫

I kept in touch with Mike's family for some years after he went on. We attended the weddings of three of his children, including Patrick. Remembering them now makes me long to reestablish contact with them. If it is right, it will happen. I believe Mike is as heartfully engaged elsewhere, on the other side, as he was when here. I have several times—and this has happened also with other friends and loved ones who have died—"seen" him in another living human being.

On one occasion, about eight months after his death, I was on the way home from the grocery store with the children and stopped for a traffic light. Several pedestrians were crossing the road directly in front of me. I was startled out of a conversation with our eldest daughter by the tall, fair-haired man walking by, a few feet away, briefcase in one hand. My heart turned over. This man was the spitting image of Mike! What was Mike doing there? The light changed, and as the car moved on I gave the man a quick, penetrating look. He was definitely not who I thought he was. Yet I swear that I saw Mike in him, if only for a minute.

Why would the dead appear to us in this way? Maybe they want to be remembered or wish to call forth in our memory the thoughts and impulses they worked for. Maybe they are asking something of us.

This brings to memory the death of another friend, also from cancer. Like Mike, Carroll went through the fire of inner and outer transformation as the disease progressed. All the unnecessary externals were burned away and her absolute trust that she was being taken care of, in both body and soul, shone forth. Her wit shone out too. Approximately fourteen years after she died in her mid-40's, I was at the vet one day waiting in line to make an appointment for our dog when I noticed a flyer on display on the counter. It was an announcement about a sixty-mile walk to raise money for breast cancer. After I'd absorbed the fact that they were looking for participants, the person in front of me moved aside and I stepped up to the receptionist. To my amazement I found myself looking into Carroll's face! She was grinning and there was a challenge in her eyes. I glanced aside at the flyer and the thought formed in me, "If you want me to do this walk, I'll do it!" When I looked back at the receptionist Carroll was gone, there was the woman I normally do business with. But I left knowing I'd committed myself to that walk, and it proved to be quite an adventure. Carroll was with me on it, reveling in the stories of cancer survivors and of loved ones who had been left behind, jokes, and the powerful mood of a common cause and camaraderie that arose among 2,500 walkers.

ANOTHER DEATH IN THE FAMILY

TWO EMOTIONS I'VE witnessed and experienced repeatedly in my encounters with both the dying and the
dead—quite apart from love, which can hardly be ade-
quately described or done justice to—are gratitude and
regret. There have been occasions when they have felt like
two sides to the same coin. One day the brightness of gratitude has prevailed and it's seemed as though the departed
are willing the sun to shine ever more brightly and directly
on their loved ones on earth. Other days there has been a
dark, inward, devouring sensation as regrets, both named
and not fully named, have emerged.

Mike, whom I described in the last chapter, often traveled back and forth between the two, both before and
after he passed over. Sometimes, when he was still on this
side and was wishing he'd done more for his family, it was
tempting to try to pacify him, to tell him everything was
just the way it was meant to be, and he'd done as much as
he could. It was Dr. Winkler, however, who made it clear
on one such occasion that I should keep my mouth shut
and allow remorse to come out in the same way that a fever
might be allowed to run its course. Then, after a day or
two, Mike's gratitude would return, made brighter yet by
the chastising, humbling powers of true self-recognition.

There were times—this chapter deals with one of them
in particular—when my own feelings of gratitude and
regret were called forth, first one, then the other, as the

mirror was held up to me too and I could feel the threads that bound me to the one who had died. Furthermore, I could feel the threads between us loosening, tightening, loosening again, and weaving onward as I thought back over our connection, pondered, marveled, asked for forgiveness, and forgave.

Cousin William came to live with our family when he was a baby. His mother had suffered a breakdown and his father couldn't manage an infant. He was the first and only child of my uncle, and was several years younger than my brother and I. I remember him in the high chair throwing peas on the floor and massaging baby food all over his head. I found him both funny and messy. Giving up my role as the youngest, the "caboose" as my father called me, may not have come easily.

William did not live with us for long—maybe a year, maybe less—but I don't think he was in the picture when I lost my hearing. Still, my brother and I spent time with him when we visited my other grandmother. There were other cousins as well, the children of my father's older brother, and we—all of us—knew William was Grandma's favorite. William knew it, too, and may have used it at times to get what he wanted. William also loved my mother very much, and I believe it was she who introduced him to his vocation—art.

A large part of my regret in this configuration, even now, is that I do not know the full story of William's life. Yes, I know that his father remarried and that William had gained an older stepbrother and stepsister who were not very nice to him. Yes, I know where he went to school and to college, how he designed and built his own house, plunged into the life of a country man, and knew a lot about woodworking, plumbing, solar energy, fruit trees, vegetable gardens, freshwater fishing, astronomy, guitar music, and much more. All while learning, experimenting, and working hard to make a living as an artist. I know that his first wife left him shortly after their daughter was born (one could not help but wonder if family history was repeating itself), and later he met and wed a wonderful woman. I also know that for years, even though we hugged each other every time we got together, shared news, and exchanged Christmas cards and gifts, I was not comfortable with him. Because of that I "dodged" him. I didn't really listen to him, although I had the feeling his gentle, kind manner sometimes masked anxiety and anger. Nor did I really share myself with him.

It's obvious that, even within our own blood family, we're more drawn to some relatives than to others—and isn't there a limit to the number of people we can be "really" open to and interested in? Isn't it sometimes easier to be interested in and loving toward those we aren't related to? Maybe so. That's the way I thought at first, but now, almost eight years after Cousin William's death, I find myself experiencing regret whenever I think of him. Perhaps it is *his* regret I'm experiencing, but before we go further into his story let me explain how he died.

Much of William's art was about the sky. He specialized in monoprints. Many of them are large—19 by 31 inches and larger (not including frames)—and have just a few inches, say 3 to 5 inches, of landscape at their base. The landscape part may include an outline of mountains in the distance, a patchwork design of farmland, or the exquisite shape of a willow beside a lake. Many of his trees look like solitary dancers pausing on stage. Yet even there you sense the trees are what they are because of the sky. William worked mostly with what I call the "in between" colors of the day, the colors of dawn and of dusk. There are pinks, peaches, and misty moist olive greens. His blues are also muted and his use of white is exceptional. In some of his pictures white-grey clouds bubble up and out of the blue like ships emerging not on the sky but from within it.

When he died William was flying an ultralight aircraft he'd assembled himself. It was the first flight—the test flight. The contraption took off and crashed in the uppermost branches of a tree, where his head slammed against the trunk. His wife, who was standing below waiting to record the event on film, had to watch the whole thing.

We were out when my mother called to tell us what had happened. The message she left on the answering machine was pretty terse: "William killed himself."

I woke early the next morning to these words said over and over, "I can't get up...? I can't get up...? I can't get up....?"

There was hardly any space between the words, they sounded more like a question than a statement, and the tone was incredibly mournful. It was the tone of someone who was trapped. In the days that followed the words continued, slowed, and eventually stopped. I got the inner impression he'd finally been able to extract himself from his body, but that release was followed by another kind of imprisonment. He longed for physical contact, primarily with his wife. He wanted to hug and hold, and longed for as much in return. There seemed to be nothing I could read, say, or do for him. Though I could sense his presence and condition, we were not really connecting. The primary sensation was one of bewilderment.

A very moving service was held for William where his wife and many of his close friends spoke from their hearts. I am certain he heard everything and that it was a consolation. A gathering at his home followed, and the physicality of that—he had always loved gatherings and good food, and there was plenty of the latter—was also, I believe, a consolation.

The time after this was pretty bleak. It was evident his wife was suffering. She lost weight and faded to a shadow of her former self. In addition to missing him, I'm sure she noticed his struggle and continued to be open to him in that way for many years, even after she remarried. William's early death was a wound to the whole family. You couldn't help but feel that, despite the creative energy he'd poured into so many different projects and his great love for his second wife, her daughter, his own daughter, and the son they had together, his life had not been easy. Something about him remained unresolved and something in him remained unfulfilled.

There's no question I *could* have been a better cousin and friend to William when he was alive. I *could* have gotten to know him in a more heartfelt manner. I *could* have made an effort to understand and transform the discomfort I felt when I was with him. Was that discomfort mine? Was it related to feelings of disdain, resentment, or envy I unknowingly harbored? Or was it something I picked up from him? Although his will worked deeply into many aspects of his everyday life (how many people design and build their own home with their own hands?), did that part of him that yearned for the sky prevent him from ever really being at home in himself on this earth? Did he really, quite unconsciously, kill himself, as my mother so bluntly put it?

The questions are endless and may, to you, seem senseless considering the fact that he's not here to answer them. But maybe he *is* here and in need of help. Maybe the questions that keep coming to me about him are really *his* questions. Maybe he's asking for something. Along these lines consider this possibility: might the recognition and admission of regret in me be of help to him? Absolutely! He may now be in a place where honesty can trigger the transformation of regret into gratitude and that, in turn, will allow him to move on to new places. Do I want to help him to move on to new places? Absolutely! Even as I write, the transformation is also occurring in *me*. The discomfort is going. I need not analyze it endlessly; I can just let it go. In its place is simple gladness that William and I were related and are still related, that I knew him, and death need not mean the end of the opportunity to continue to get to know him.

THE NIGHT WATCHMAN

FOR ALMOST A year I wrote a column for a hospice newsletter. I interviewed nurses, volunteers, a doctor, a nurse practitioner, a pastor, a receptionist, a director, and the night watchman. The purpose of the column was to help folks in that community to get to know one another, so most of the questions had to do with the person's background, family, hobbies and such, rather than their actual work—although if they wanted to speak about their work, they did. Many had moving stories to tell of their experiences with the patients and the families of the patients. With all of them I felt a sincere wish to help alleviate pain however they could, be it physical, emotional, or spiritual, so the death experience would be as smooth as possible and free of trauma.

The last interview, the one with the night watchman, was, for me, the most profound. Curiously, I was scheduled to interview a doctor, not this man. When I got there, I learned the doctor was at the hospital and couldn't meet, so I looked around for someone else, and there was Daniel. Curiously too, my final interview was never published. The editor didn't explain why. Perhaps, in their view, Daniel was not "professional" or "educated" enough. He had barely made it through high school and didn't speak proper English. He was also missing a front tooth, which was a source of embarrassment, and he really had to struggle to express himself, though he had much to say. Shortly after I submitted the profile, the editor left for another job, the organization went through an overhaul, and I stopped writing for them.

Daniel was in his mid-sixties when I met him and, with his bristly grey hair, looked very much the grandfather he was. The thoughtful silence in his brown eyes caught my attention. Words waited in those eyes. I was also struck by the fact that, for a stocky man, he had unusually slender, sensitive hands.

Daniel plunged right into the story of his wife's battle with breast cancer and her completely unexpected death sixteen years earlier. He was hard to lip read, because of the missing tooth, but his face was wide open. He said that for a year after her death he was totally confused, could not come to grips with the fact that the person he loved the most had been taken from him, and did nothing. He spoke of having "flashes," glimpses of his wife, which he worried were hallucinations related to his loneliness. He considered going to a doctor but never did, because the "flashes" brought him pleasure. Were they "right"? Were they "wrong"? What was going on? He confided in no one because he was ashamed of his own confusion and didn't want his family thinking he'd gone crazy.

Daniel paused at this point and gave me an anxious look. I realized he was asking me not to include anything about his apparently unusual perceptions in the article. I assured him that what he was telling me was off the record. (This was not the first time this had happened when I was interviewing there. One of the nurses had blurted out that she was a "white witch" who secretly prayed for help while administering medications, often seeing angelic beings standing beside the beds of dying patients.)

Daniel said he next found himself responding to an ad for a plainclothes security officer at hospice, work he'd never done or considered doing before then. Nor did he know much about hospice, though he was struck by how very "right" the job felt when he came for the interview. At this point I sensed a feminine presence with us. I believe the wife was there then too, participating in our interview, nodding eagerly, suggesting that it was she who had drawn his attention to the ad.

Daniel's confidence grew as he shared his story. It came as no surprise that he was quite aware of the presence of the dead both inside and outside the building. He spoke a bit about the different personalities and the need of some to stay around for a while after their body had been cremated and their beds filled. It amused him that the building had to be locked at night when locks obviously mattered not at all to those no longer in the body. I felt he was being guided not only by his essential goodness and by his wife, but also by a very basic, instinctive wisdom.

One thing I kept hearing during that conversation was Daniel's heightened awareness of the moment of death. Without having to be near any of the patients, he "knew" when they were leaving. I suspect he was a watchman in more ways than one, and this sensitivity was quite amazingly demonstrated toward the end of our conversation.

Forty minutes into the interview Daniel interrupted himself to exclaim, "I *know* someone in my family died two hours ago!"

He spoke of his father's brother's son, whom he hadn't seen in over twenty years.

"Are you talking about a cousin?" I asked.

Slightly impatient, he replied, "My father's brother's son... he was a veteran... had diabetes... lives in the South."

"And you said he died two hours ago?"

"I *know* he died... I saw it. I'm gonna to go home... I'm gonna get a phone call telling me he's dead."

Then he added with a tinge of annoyance, "Guess I'll have to go to that funeral... watch everyone blabbering and drinking." He made it sound as though funerals were more for those left behind than for those who had gone on.

This conversation meant a great deal to me. It was the first one I'd had in that environment where it was a taken fact that the dead are all around and have needs, preferences, and even agendas after passing over. It was an immense relief to talk with someone who, while being fully aware of pain, was not focused primarily on pain. I believe that night watchman was placed there to act as a witness. For the dead, like the living, need to know their passages are seen, heard, felt, shared, and honored.

This may sound strange, but it was as though Daniel was urging me to shift my attention from the crucifixion aspect of death to the resurrection forces within each death. I would have stopped writing the column then, even if asked to continue, because my sojourn there was over. This was over ten years ago, and I believe attitudes toward the dead and the whole process of dying are already different now from what they were then.

Something happened that day after the interview with Daniel, which I felt he was responsible for. It was late July, and after leaving the center I took our dog for a brief walk before heading home. I'd parked at the far end of the parking lot near a slope on which rows of mature white pines grew. The dog and I climbed the slope, made our way through the pine growth, and found a meadow on the other side. I'd never known it was there.

It was a glorious summer day, not too hot or humid, in fact just right. The meadow was abloom with brown-eyed Susans, Queen Anne's lace, butterfly weed, flowering grasses, and more. As we waded into it the dog's tail swished this way and that up ahead like a great feather opening a path, and a jumble of images and impressions rushed toward me.

I saw the light of the sun calling forth not only the flowers, but also beings around and within them. Colors and forms sang to one another and jostled playfully. One minute, sights predominated, the next, scents. The plants spoke through perfume as well as hue.

Then I became aware of yet another dimension. I heard what I knew were the voices of dead souls who had left the building I'd stepped out of minutes before.

"My gosh! Come here..."

"Hey, look at this!"

"Did you ever?"

It sounded like an intoxicated gathering. The mood was celebratory, similar to some graduation parties I've attended.

As I stood there trying to take it all in—and my wakefulness only lasted about five to eight minutes—one feeling emerged above the others: the dead may be burdened by confusion, regrets and unfinished business, just as we are, but it is also possible for the moment of death to be experienced as a glorious opening. An opening out beyond walls, roofs, clocks, rules, schedules, and locks, into the pulse of divine life.

PART II

JOHN

$\mathscr{A}$ Few Thoughts

before the Next Story

As I hope I've made clear in the earlier chapters, the nature and quality of our relationship with a person on this side figures strongly into the nature and quality of our relationship with that person when he or she has passed over. I've found that remembering moments when I really met and was with a person when he or she was here can set the tone for meetings with that person after death. The intensity and purity of the feelings seem to be the key. For example, I might call up the gratitude and love I felt in the middle of a particular conversation I had with this person and may then sense what I call "the responding chord." It's as though I've whistled a note in the dark and the whistle has been returned. The whistle comes not as echo but response, and the response grows stronger and more definite as I allow myself to go deeper into the gratitude and love. Recalling the place, the time of year and day, the facial expressions, and a myriad of other details is very much a part of this grateful re-membering. It is also possible to connect when remembering or rereading written exchanges and the feelings that accompanied them. I suppose it can occur when recalling telephone conversations, too.

At the same time I believe it's important to keep in mind that gratitude and love, if not properly cultivated and guarded, can turn into sentimental nostalgia, unhealthy longing, even resentment over separation. Those are *not* of help to the departed and *don't* make for real connections. They are like cul-de-sacs. We can know if we're trapped in them because there is no sense of movement. Our relationship with the deceased, if it is to be meaningful and alive, needs to be every bit as responsive to changes as it was when we were together on this side. There's a paradox in the fact that while we may connect by way of memories, we do not want to be stuck in mere memory of the other.

There are some very beautiful aspects to the fact that the life we knew on this side with another can remain an integral part of the "weave" of our life and our relationship with that soul after he or she has crossed over. For example, remembering that this person was interested in history, loved art or classical music, or had greatly enjoyed travel in a certain part of the world, can awaken new interests and abilities in us. Those who have departed can become our guides as we open to what they loved while they were here. They may even seek to become further involved in these interests through us and may seem to "engineer" meetings we have with people on this side, as I'll try to illustrate in the pages ahead.

Another aspect of the continuing "weave" of our life with the life of the one who has passed over may come in the realization that we knew this person in a different incarnation, or in several different incarnations. Perhaps we knew or sensed this when together this time around, and then more dimensions of these other lives become evident after our friend has gone on. I think the weaving analogy really expresses it wonderfully. If you've ever closely examined woven fabric with a complex pattern of many colors you will know what I'm trying to say. You might see how one color seems to disappear, reappear, and disappear again. You might see too how the underside of the weave is a beautiful and mysterious counterpart of the upper side. What "disappeared" on the upper side is often very much in evidence when the fabric is turned over. In every day life on this side we may think our loved one is gone, but when we reach out, sense a response, and try to connect, we may be granted glimpses of the other side of the heart weaving we are doing together.

JOHN ON THIS SIDE

I MET JOHN IN the spring of my twenty-third year. Dr. Winkler had, through another person, directed me to visit a Waldorf school. John was the leader of this school and director of the teacher training program there, which is what I went to see.

When I stepped into the school I experienced a feeling I'd never known before. It can only be expressed in the words, "This is where I'm meant to be!" Tears welled up in my eyes. Then the feeling passed and I went to the classroom where other young people my age were gathered.

Minutes later John walked in. Fifty-four years old at the time, he was tall, carried himself with an air of nobility, had a broad forehead, wavy brown hair with a whisper of silver-white, and a relaxed, humorous smile that reminded me of the comedian Jack Benny. His blue eyes listened carefully. It was the way he moved his hands that stayed with me when I thought back on the visit later that day. He appeared to be sculpting thoughts out of the air as he talked. Sometimes he'd raise the index finger of his right hand, but not in a pedantic manner. The finger seemed to say, "Listen with me" or, "Let's be open to this other possibility" or even, "That must be it!" While this finger was extremely articulate, his hands were in no way hurried or impatient. Rather, they were generous and unpretentious. Later, when I came to know his handwriting I marveled that such large hands, the hands of a wood splitter, trail blazer, and gardener, as well as an educator, could make such small, precise, neat letters.

After the class I went with the other student teachers to lunch in the cafeteria. Toward the end of the meal John came over to tell me he wanted to have a few words in his office. I nearly fell over when I entered that space, for there on the shelf behind his desk was a photo of my maternal grandfather! It turned out they'd been good friends for some time before my grandfather's death fifteen years earlier. John had known all along of the connection but had chosen to say nothing about it until that moment.

The outcome of the conversation that followed was that I applied to and then enrolled in the one-year teacher training program. It was a wonderful year, although John called up some pretty contrary elements in me. When he told me I needed to change my handwriting I flat-out refused to do anything about it. When he suggested I wear longer skirts, I also refused. (Looking now at photographs of those times I wonder how I got away with that one.) When Edward and I became engaged that November, John said he thought it would be a good idea to wait until the following June to get married. I came close to blowing up. Who was he to tell us when to have our wedding? (We were married in April.) Whatever annoyances I felt toward John did not, however, last long, because I enjoyed sparring with him. Our disagreements were really over minor things. On a higher level I was tremendously challenged by his way of talking, thinking, and interpreting the insights of Rudolf Steiner. Challenging is the first word that comes to me when I think of words that best catch the essence of John. Rigorous, discerning, disciplined, fearless, supportive, and loyal are others.

Edward and I moved away the next year. I continued to read Steiner and would write John long letters full of philosophical ruminations and endless questions. He always responded. I remember one exchange in particular at this time. I asked why Steiner wasn't better known, particularly when the world seemed to be in such a sorry state. John wrote:

> Depression causes us to view things dubiously and darkly, but does it go so far as to make you doubt that grass is green? Much of what Steiner has to say is of that order. It should make sense in or out of depression.
>
> When I hear Steiner's name used more than once or twice, I get nervous. He is not in question, does not make himself an issue, does not call attention to himself. He is great because he finds the world great, nature great, history great, art-science-religion-education-bees and cow manure and all earth processes great. Above all, he directs attention and builds the bridge of thought and feeling to Christ. If you know a better path to Christ, for example, the Gospels, use it when the going gets tough.

I was startled by John's use of the word *depression*. Did he think *I* was depressed? I was startled also by his mention of Christ. He had never brought up the name in conversation with me before. Something in my heart stirred—for what I wasn't sure. My response to that letter was to prove that, of course, I *wasn't* depressed, I was very busy, happily married, and all that. Like, Dr. Winkler, though, John could perceive the different soul natures remarkably clearly. He knew my happiness depended on my ability to connect with the best and highest in myself and in the world. He made his point in a subsequent letter where he stated that the three important things in life are: 1) finding one's work, 2) finding one's mate, and 3) finding one's relationship to God. He underlined that last one.

Another year and a half passed and we moved back to John's area. He offered Edward a job teaching, which Edward accepted. Close to twenty-five years later, when Edward was himself the head of a school and was discussing a possible candidate for a job, John recalled that time, and the amount of thought he gave to his offer. He said it's a major, sometimes even a dangerous, thing to step into another person's karma.

I believe that comment goes a long way in illustrating John's belief in the importance of watching and praying. He believed in praying, not for things to happen or not happen because such praying in his opinion was a form of mistrust ("God knows far better than I what is needed"), but for guidance ("Show me what I must and can do"). His watchfulness was evident in his interest in all forms of life. One time during the intermission at a school play I noticed him gazing intently at something, went over, and asked what had caught his attention. He was pondering the shape of the ears of the man seated in front of him, and proceeded to describe how different lobes reveal different personality characteristics. John was always looking for the divine script as events unfolded locally, nationally, and universally. He was also particularly interested in the dreams and out-of-the-ordinary experiences many shared with him. His attentiveness moved back and forth with great agility and with discerning power between inner states of being and outer manifestations. Through such listening he exemplified the leading (or drawing out) power of the true educator. There were moments when I knew he was helping me to create myself, and my life, as he listened, in person and in his letters.

Two other aspects of John's trust in the highest can be found in two quotations he often cited, especially later in his life. The first appears in a passage from Steiner's book *Theosophy*. I've italicized the part he would cite:

Seekers of knowledge cannot consider only what will yield fruit or lead to success for themselves; they must also consider what they have recognized as good. They must willingly submit to the strict law that requires them to renounce all personal arbitrariness and all fruits their actions may have for their own personality. Then they are walking the paths of the spiritual world and their whole being is permeated by its laws. They are freed from all sensory constraints; their spirit being lifts free of its sensory trappings. This is how they spiritualize themselves, how they make progress toward the spiritual.

We cannot question whether it does any good to resolve to obey only the laws of truth when in fact we may be mistaken about what is true. Everything depends on our effort and our attitude, and even people who are mistaken but are aspiring to the truth possess a strength that will set them back on the right track. The very objection that we may be mistaken is in itself destructive disbelief and demonstrates a lack of trust in the power of truth. (pp. 188–189)

The second quotation is from St. Augustine: "Love God and do what you will."

It's tempting to speak at length about John's life, interests, friendships, accomplishments, and more. I know that people who knew him and read this will feel my picture is not the whole picture. It isn't. The goal here is not to write a biography but to provide a sketch of John and certain events that involved us both because those events are directly related to the purpose of this book.

The True, for John, as portrayed in the quote from Steiner, was, in essence, the Divine. John's manner of speaking was, however, never dogmatic or theological. It always came out of the liveliness of his own mind and the certainty and wonder of his own heart. For example, he looked for the best in two quite different paths, Charismatic Christianity and Anthroposophy, and tried to articulate what he believed they had to offer one another. He read widely and deeply in search of the True. Furthermore, he not only lived for it, but *gave* his life in service to it. This really shaped the school he led. It was an exciting place to be. When we were there, Edward and I felt connected to an extraordinary impulse and an extraordinary community. Others spoke of it as a Camelot—though the sad part is that John's interpretation of what was True later split the place apart.

Edward worked for eight years at John's school. During that time I taught deaf children elsewhere and our daughters were born. I saw John quite regularly at school events, showed him poems and stories I'd written, and we often socialized with him and his wonderful wife, Carol, whom I came to regard as a second mother.

In October of Edward's ninth year there the community became embroiled over the presence of a young man John had befriended. Richard was highly clairvoyant, but some were not interested in or open to his perceptions. To best summarize the outcome of a story that cannot be gone into in depth and with justice here, John and anyone who had consulted with Richard were asked to leave the school. Edward was among those who departed, because both of us had had several conversations with Richard.

This turn of events led John and Carol to relocate. Our own experiences with Richard continued for a few years after Edward left this Waldorf school. Richard pointed out the way to me. It is because of him I experienced an awakening to the presence of a loving being with whom I conversed for almost three years. I recorded that conversation as best as I could in half a dozen or more journals.

These experiences really cemented our connection with John, although we lived several hours apart.

I will always be grateful to John for introducing me to Richard. John had known all along that I would indeed encounter depression if I couldn't find and enter into an active relationship with the spiritual world. It was not simply a matter of remembering I'd heard an inner voice as a child or young person; it was a matter of finding, turning to, and awakening to it again, and again, and again.

In our renewed correspondence John repeatedly wrote that he himself wasn't clairvoyant. I never took his words seriously, because I believe we limit ourselves when we assume clairvoyance and clairaudience only mean seeing visions and hearing voices. *Everyone* is capable of having supersensible and intuitive perceptions, which often suggest the beginnings of clairvoyance, and one may in fact be having them without recognizing them for what they are. Furthermore, such perceptions may arise not only spontaneously but out of the presence and conscious cultivation of certain attitudes and feelings. John's ability to recognize and salute the spirit in others, as well as in events, was rooted in his reverence for the True. Reverence enabled him to see more than most. As I heard within,

> A. (John) cannot see with clairvoyance
> yet he can see through the reverence in his heart.
> His reverence is an organ of perception,
> it is there whether he knows it or not.
> So can it be with all of you. (*Becoming*, p. 140)

With some encouragement, John later began recording words he himself heard inwardly. He was extremely modest about these gems which he shared with close friends. As they offer glimpses into the trials he was subject to at that time, here are three:

In all things praise God:
in sorrow as in joy,
in loneliness as in companionship,
in defeat as in victory.
Both belong to God;
He uses the dark to strengthen your experience of
    the light.

My message to you and all your friends is "Abide."
Abide through thick and thin, high and low, dark
    and light.
He comes to see how all is for the best who has first,
before he could see, abided in trust in me and our
    Father.
There are reasons why everything does not always
    seem to go well,
but the loving wisdom behind those reasons
is made known only to those whose faith does not
    rest on reasons.

Be glad! The time of testing is here.
Hold firm, abide quietly in trust
and good will; see my victory unfold.
The old must be done away with, but
Behold, I will make all things new!

Thirteen years after John left the Waldorf School he
was advised by Richard to bring together a group of people who wished to serve the world and Christ in particular. Richard was never a part of this gathering, though
the impetus for starting it came from him. Edward and I
were among those invited. I was then guided to share with

these people the verses from my journals, which had been packed away, forgotten, in the back of my closet.

It was John who said the verses should be published. Together we went through them, page by page, asking for help editing, clarifying, and arranging. The fruit of that collaboration was the book *Turning*. John's respect for the material I'd received years before and his ability to find layers of meanings within it not only gave me new confidence in what I'd heard, but opened the door for more to come. For seven years I inwardly heard on behalf of John and the group he'd gathered. The fruit of that is the sequel to *Turning*, published under the title *Becoming*.

It was a privilege and a joy to work with John in this way. Though we lived several hours apart, depended on the mail service to communicate (this was before email was available), and were both busy where we lived, there was an amazing degree of intimacy to the work. He could go to sleep in the evening with a question on his mind and I could wake in the morning receiving thoughts that later, we both realized, were the answer to his question. Sometimes I'd send him a letter and his response to the thoughts I'd expressed would arrive the next day as my envelope was being put in his mailbox. He eventually got a fax machine (we already had one) to speed up the communications. I could also pick up on difficulties he was having and he, in turn, was sensitive to the ups and downs in Edward's work and in the lives of our daughters.

Over a period of about fourteen years I had two vivid, detailed, dreamlike experiences of being in another time and culture with John. They occurred over several days. It was almost like watching a movie trilogy. In both experiences his face was the face of a stranger, but in the first I instantly "recognized" him by way of the feelings he called up, and in the second the recognition occurred the minute I saw this person's hand movements. Though my deceased grandmother believed in reincarnation, I'd never discussed it with her and my own parents were not open to the topic. My father dismissed it quite a few times as a form of narcissism, and while his argument made sense to me, the possibility of reincarnation made even more sense to me. For one thing, I simply could not deny the experiences I'd had. (There had been others besides the ones I had with John, though not quite as detailed.) For another, my experience from an early age of sleeping and waking was such that I sometimes was aware of the movement out of and back into my body. Occasionally I'd hear a "whooshing" sound as though I was swirling down a chute back into the physical world at high speed. That I went out of my body at night, that the fatigue that had accumulated during the previous day was apparently washed away and I was filled with new strength was, and is still, a source of grateful wonderment. Because of this I came to believe, on my own, that the daily ritual of sleeping and waking is a small-scale model of a much larger activity that occurs over and over, when we die and later are reborn.

I had always been puzzled by the fierce negative reactions the idea of reincarnation calls up in some people. John was the first person I talked with in depth about all of this. It was a tremendous relief to share my experiences with him and to know I was heard and would not be judged, teased, or ridiculed. He was extremely interested in possible past life experiences and connections, more so than I. Occasionally his interest in the topic was so pronounced it brought up the contrariness mentioned earlier. When he "got going" about such possibilities, my reaction was often, "So what? We're here now." I don't want to sound disrespectful of his beliefs, which were altogether sincere, but felt on more than one occasion, when he was speaking of his conviction that so-and-so had been so-and-so in a previous life, that his words were putting an enormous weight on that person. I tried to be honest about this, and also about my discomfort when he spoke of "dark forces." John wasn't prone to conspiracy theories but did believe there were beings that wanted to thwart the good work. At that time I didn't give much thought to his words. Now that I'm older I'm more open to that possibility.

John and I felt ourselves to be at the service of the Christ impulse. John said he believed the voice of Christ was speaking through *Turning*, and I was, quite frankly, overwhelmed by the possibility. To this day I alternate between joy and discomfort when I think of that prospect. True, I have since the creation of *Turning* read beautiful accounts by Gabrielle Bossis (*He and I*) and Nicole Gausseron (*The Little Notebooks*) and their conversations with Jesus. I've also read profound messages heard by unnamed others, as evidenced in *God Calling* and *Listen, the Lord*, so I know many hear within. However, when a name is attached to what is heard, when the attention shifts from the life in the words to the One who speaks them, I feel very small indeed. When I tried to express this to John he nodded gravely and admitted it was easy for him to talk about *Turning*, but when he considered the source of the verses in his journals he became wordless. Some years later when he and I were reading aloud from the Gospel of St. John we were both, at the end of each chapter, struck wordless for about half an hour. This happened several days in a row. We never discussed it when he was here, on this side, but later, after he'd passed over, he referred to it. I'll speak of it in the next section.

I was completely in accord with John's belief in what he took to calling the Direct Approach. The name comes from an entry in *Turning:*

> There is no substitute for the direct approach
>   to me.
> Everyone must do it alone,
> Not through anyone else. (p. 41)

The forthrightness of the Direct Approach seemed clean and simple, and to this day it remains almost a natural reflex in my interior life when I'm discouraged or perplexed or need guidance. I ask as simply and directly as I can, any time, anywhere, in any situation, for help. The asking may or may not be accompanied by inner pictures. Answers *always* come, though not always right away (sometimes days, months, or years later) or in words heard inwardly (sometimes in inner pictures or through the words or actions of others). Many in John's group had beautiful stories to tell of their experiences using this approach.

However, questions arose in connection with the Direct Approach as we sought to use it not just individually but as a group. What happens when several people get different answers to the same question? What if a person seems, unconsciously, to be using it to forward a personal agenda? (I was already bothered by the example of certain fundamentalists who do things, sometimes very unloving things, claiming God "told" them to act in this manner.) Do some people hear the inner word more loudly and accurately than others? In retrospect I think the questions were and still are symptomatic of our times. They're an important part of the process of finding a true working relationship with the supersensible worlds. I personally found these questions hard because inner hearing has always, for me, been a private, interior experience, and while I wholeheartedly embraced the belief that anyone can experience inner hearing, I didn't want to be called upon to judge what others are hearing.

John was different. He was eager to hear from everybody and listened to what we received inwardly in utmost seriousness. He was also, primarily, a man of action. He urged us to act on what we heard, for he knew guidance is given to the degree that it's taken and used. Why should the supersensible world keep sending messages if you aren't going to open, read, and make use of them? If your mailbox is stuffed full of unopened letters, well, then it'll look for someone else to communicate with. When Edward and I connected with others in John's area interested in starting a school based on the Direct Approach, we decided to take the plunge. We attended meetings, often weekly, for over a year. Then Edward left his job, we dipped into our savings, and put our house on the market.

It was an exciting and scary time. Hearing beautiful words within was one thing. Wondering how they were going to translate into making a living, let alone creating a whole new school, was something else.

One morning when talking with John, I burst into tears and likened the whole enterprise to a wobbly, shifting bowl of Jell-O.

He regarded me calmly before asking, "Where's your faith?"

"Where are the students?" I sobbed back. "Where's the faculty? Where's the building to house the whole thing? Where's the money?"

Unruffled, John gave his bright-funny Jack Benny smile. This was the only time in the years I knew him when I experienced his presence as overbearing. I felt he was pushing us in a way that was uncalled for and said so. I explained how we, and our wonderful, unwavering co-worker Debbie, were attending the meetings, he was not, and did not really know the other folks involved. In short, he didn't know the particulars, the picture as we saw it up close; he was focused only on the big vision.

John apologized, stepped back, and then came on even stronger. I believe he was right *and* we were right, and somehow we were having trouble integrating the two views and the information from each—from what was in front of us and from the words, dreams, and nudges received within in silence and prayer.

I hated the tightness and tension between John and us at this time and remember asking him to please stop talking about the Direct Approach, as though it was a mantra he repeated endlessly to anyone. I also was concerned about his health. He'd had stomach problems off and on for several months, and had lost weight.

John came across a book at this time and urged me to read it. In *The Book of Theanna: In the Lands that Follow Death*, Ellias Lonsdale describes his communications with his wife after she died. When this book was put into my hands I had a strong reaction. Tears rose to my eyes, similar to when I'd first stepped into the Waldorf School. I had to sit down to recollect myself. After that, I could read the book only in small doses. John made it clear both in person and in his letters that he wanted very much for us to remain connected after he passed on. We intuitively knew this was coming sooner, rather than later. He said, to others as well as to me, that he thought he might be more helpful on the other side than here. Yet the awareness that his time was approaching undoubtedly contributed to his over-involvement in our school project. John and I had also read and discussed lectures by Steiner on life after death. It was the influence of Steiner rather than Ellias Lonsdale that led me to say, "I'll do what I can to stay connected with you, but, really, I can't promise anything." He seemed satisfied with that.

John was in and out of the hospital the spring of the year he died. The first time he was hospitalized he was told he was anemic and needed a blood transfusion. He said he didn't want anybody else's blood in his body. When I suggested a gift was being offered in the form of the transfusion, John changed his mind and got it. After that it became evident that a curious push-pull dynamic had been set in motion that seemed quite alien to the decisive man we'd known for thirty-one years.

About two weeks after the blood transfusion, John had a stroke. He suffered from mild facial paralysis and his speech was affected. That he couldn't talk easily was a source of immense frustration, as it was evident there were thoughts he desperately wanted to share. Later he had other mini-strokes, was unable to swallow, and had to be fed through a feeding tube. Since Carol couldn't look after him as closely as his condition required, he was moved to a nursing home. A steady stream of visitors from the different phases of his life came to talk with him. The staff said they had never seen anything like it, and John enjoyed it all, though he sometimes asked afterward who the people were. He also made friends among the nurses, gave away copies of *Turning*, and made sure they knew about the Direct Approach.

The last month was extremely difficult. John's body was deteriorating, and he was bedridden except for a couple of hours daily, when he sat in a wheelchair in his room or in the lounge. Some who were close to him wondered if he was in his right mind, because he referred to meetings he expected to attend or had attended, got dates, times, and people mixed up; and spoke of strange animals and other creatures. It's my belief he was straddling the two worlds.

One evening when I came in, I saw he had soiled himself and would need to be cleaned. He took one look at me, shut his eyes, and retreated within himself. I felt his shame. When I took his hand and held it with both of mine his mouth trembled as he said, "I've *never* experienced anything like this before!"

Another time, also in the evening, I sat beside him, marveled at the blueness of his eyes and was glad we didn't have to talk. When I got up to leave I asked, "Are you going to be here tomorrow?"

He smiled. "Probably."

"What are you thinking?"

He smiled again and made an upward motion with the open palm of one hand. "I'm thinking God created us because He wanted to learn about Himself."

The next morning was quite different. He was tossing about. Again I took his hand and he held mine so tightly it hurt. When I got up to leave he let go reluctantly with the words, "I hope there will soon be an end to these incomprehensible events."

There were days when I couldn't "find" him, when he was either looking beyond us all at the other world, or lying motionless with his eyes shut, apparently asleep. I know the staff gave him tranquilizers because he sometimes had to be restrained. When this first happened I was so bothered by it I begged him silently to let go and get on. He was responding less and less, though his bright smile flashed forth once or twice when, as I was saying good-bye, I clasped both hands together and raised them high. He had regularly, in the past, given us this triumphant high hand clasp when we were leaving his home. I'd always understood it to be an expression of solidarity, and wanted him to know we were with him then.

One day while driving down the hill from our house I entreated God to put an end to John's suffering. As I finished the prayer a red-tailed hawk swooped down right over the car from behind and, flying just inches from the hood, led the way through an archway of tall, leafy trees. The bird flew straight up into the sky and disappeared as I came out into the open landscape and sunlight. In my heart I knew John wasn't quite ready to go, there was more he needed to experience, and when the time came he'd soar right into the light.

A few hours later I heard these words:

> John has given you courage,
> exquisite courage,
> all these years,
> courage to believe in what can be heard and seen
> within.
>
> Now you must find that courage
> —in yourself.

It was a solemn moment and a profound reminder that even in the midst of John's travail, other beings whom I could not see were aware of all that was going on, and not only in him but in everyone connected to him.

There was an emergency visit to the hospital in the last week when he was in acute pain from an intestinal obstruction. We both, and Carol, wondered how there could be an obstruction when he hadn't eaten any solid food for so long. In accordance with the living will he'd signed some years before, Carol told them not to operate, and he was returned to the nursing home under heavy sedation. We were certain he was going to die that night.

Two days later, on John's eighty-sixth birthday, four friends and Edward and I sat outside in a circle behind the nursing home. We sang his favorite songs, and spoke directly to his spirit, thanking him for being the teacher and friend he'd been to each of us. We also remembered how he'd once said he liked nothing more than bringing good friends together, and in the spirit of that comment went to his room, stood around his bed, and thanked him again. To outer appearance he was asleep.

During this final week I had no inner contact with John. This bothered me, but the wonder of the hawk that had led the way through the dark, leafy archway was so strong, I knew I should not let personal feelings of bewilderment or loss color the moment. And still he held on, both pulling at life and pushing it away.

Carol was stalwart throughout the ordeal of that last month. We visited daily, sometimes more than once a day. As we were unable to talk with John about his condition, she wondered if homeopathic assistance might make the transition easier for him. A doctor friend, learning of her thoughts, delivered a remedy to her one morning just as we were leaving for the nursing home.

John lay slumped over himself, eyes open, then shut, then open, seemingly unfocused. His mouth was partially open. His long limbs were in loose, casual array. His familiar hands looked more like large, discarded gloves than hands. His hair, which had been snow-white for close to twenty years, was still thick and wavy. His feet were turning blue. Carol put the homeopathic pellets on his tongue, after which the nurse said she was going to wash him, so we tiptoed out.

The last words we heard from John that day were, "Come here…. Come please…. Come now…."

JOHN ON THE OTHER SIDE

EARLY IN THE morning of the day after John died I had a dream. In the dream I walked into a room and there on a table was a plate piled high with cookies. John was standing beside the table discoursing. I thought, "Woops! Edward wrote an obituary for you yesterday!"

John was very much there and very well. The left side of his mouth, the side that had been affected by the stroke, was fine. Though he was evidently speaking to others—whom I couldn't see—he turned, looked directly at me, smiled, and glanced down at the cookies with a nod. He was inviting me to have some. I woke up laughing. He'd had quite a sweet tooth.

The wake was held in his home. It was wonderful to sit beside the coffin in the quiet of the room in which he wrote, read, and had private conversations with family and friends. He felt very close, but I heard nothing until the middle of the funeral three days later when an old friend of his was reminiscing. First I sensed an air of impatience and disbelief, then I inwardly heard him exclaim quite loudly, "She's talking about me as if I'm dead!"

I exalted in those words. After the bizarre month and a half in the hospital and the nursing home, John sounded as though he was himself again, and zesty as ever! In fact there was an air of euphoria around him for about ten days after his passing. I felt it, too.

Both Edward and I got the strong impression he wished to be read to and wanted, in particular, to hear the words of Ralph Waldo Emerson. John had been close to Emerson during his life. He wrote about him, had a photograph of him on the wall in his study, and said he thought of him as a relative. We read several essays by Emerson over a period of about three weeks and found ourselves being drawn into an enjoyment we believe was his as well as our own. To this day we can't read Emerson without thinking of him.

I heard clear, sometimes urgent, words from John during the next six months. It was as though he was still connected to his vocal organs and word-forming abilities and wanted to make as much use of them as possible before that particular form of communicating fell away and dissolved. I'll share some of those messages. After that, a phase of about six years followed during which, because of certain incidents, I came to understand that John was trying to glean as much as he could from parts of his life review. I was involved in some of this. During this time, his sentences were much shorter, and more energy and attentiveness were required of me when it came to translating them and the inner impressions and feelings I received from him. This is still the case. Then, almost two and a half years ago, I understood that my help was not needed in the same way and the relationship was changing. It's still changing.

The note of urgency I mentioned came through early on. Seven days after John's death I heard these words addressed not only to me but to mutual friends: "I long to see in you all the flourishing and growth of thought into action. I don't want you to spend your time repeating thoughts I've passed on to you. Don't hold me in the thought patterns you associated with me on earth. There is too little time—as you know it—for that. Through your thought-infused actions I can find and maintain contact with you."

He urged us to "Leave no leaf unturned" in our search for Christ; stressed the importance of attempting to awaken to "loving perception" of this world and its events, especially the apparently "disastrous" events; and spoke gravely of the power of words and how they are used, and of the difference between "head thinking" and "heart thinking." I felt John's disappointment as a hollow, empty feeling in my stomach when he spoke of the failure of those who think they love others, both family and friends, yet flat-out fail, again and again, to be encouraging and supportive of these others. On several occasions he offered me a far more fair and generous view of certain people we both knew. I have to say I personally felt ashamed every time this happened, but there was never any condemnation from him.

About a month after John died, a doctor friend expressed his amazement that his end had been so difficult. This friend said he assumed that John, being a spiritually developed person, would have had a smoother, quicker transition. As he was talking I sensed John right there, raring to get in a few words! The gist of what he had to say was that he was glad to have gained insight into the sufferings of others who have experienced strokes and other prolonged physical breakdowns, as well as a better understanding of some of the connections between the physical, etheric, and astral realms. He sounded rather scientific. Like Dr. Winkler, John expressed dismay over the path of modern medicine. The implication was that morally and ethically we lag way behind our intellectual, medical achievements.

Concerning my missing John's physical presence and having moments when I doubted that I was really connecting with him, he offered quite a range of responses. One day he said it was important that I not dwell on his physical absence. My missing him in that way could prevent him from getting on with things he needed to do. He said to keep love flowing outward to the world, to the natural world and its beauty and wonders, if it was an effort for me to communicate verbally with people; otherwise the flow would be reversed, would suck inward and become self-pity.

Then, a day later, during a difficult moment in a meeting, I felt his hand come down gently over mine. I felt protected, secure, and understood.

Yet another time John said,

> There is a balm—
> an ointment, a salve, a nectar—
> which can soothe this great sense of loss.
> He dispenses it—
> you are not even aware of it,
> but He does.
> Believe me,
> He does and He will.
> His mercy is infinite.
> How else can love go on?

Another day when I was missing his Jack Benny smile and was on the way to get my hair trimmed, I was suddenly certain he was in the front passenger seat, and heard this brief, hilarious remark, "Well, *I* was no great beauty!"

And another day when I was feeling vulnerable and inadequate and was wondering how Edward and I would manage without his good advice, I heard: "Do what you do best."

I think it is normal for those on this side to wonder if they really are connecting with those who have passed over. This can be compounded by waking in the morning to the feeling you've been talking all night with the one who has died, yet can't remember a word of what was said or what was discussed. The feeling grows in one that it's all a dream. John and I actually talked about this before he died, yet even I was, and still am, prey to doubt. John sometimes impressed, and continues to impress, the reality of his presence on me with these words—or with the very definite feeling that accompanies them—both in dreams and when I'm awake: "I *am* here!" It's almost as though he's trying, quickly and boldly, to out-shout my mind before it can begin questioning the authenticity of the moment and the exchanges.

Shortly after he passed over, John addressed this matter of doubt and also confirmed the intimate, inward nature of listening to the deceased. I wrote of this in the book *Friend of My Heart,* as follows:

One day I found myself thinking of him, picturing him, asking silently, "How is it for you?" Quite early the next morning I woke hearing these words:

How is it for you? That is also my question to YOU! Your heart listening to mine becomes my heart listening to yours. If you are alert to the nature of your own comments and questions to me you will find many of them are mine to you. Thus do hearts converse together, within one another, and the search of each for words, pictures, and other forms of living expression becomes a mutual search to bridge the gap between life and death. Don't let your mind separate us, don't let it get going with, "What am I doing wrong?" or, as you are wondering right this minute, "Am I making this all up?" (p. 149)

John has also spoken several times of the value of meeting "in the silence." My understanding of this, and I've spoken of it in earlier chapters, is that the dead, like the living, need times of simply, quietly "being together" with us. The minutes of silence privately and publicly offered up in remembrance of the dead *are* important. When it happens with John it's as though he's saying, "Leave all your worries and questions outside on the doorstep for awhile—it's not that I'm not interested in them, but let's have some time without them, basking in the sunshine." And the "sunshine" for him may be the warmth of love that I and others are sending to him. Even as we, on this side, have moments when a thoughtful gesture or act of kindness from another can turn an apparently grey day into a clear and hopeful one, the dead can also experience a climatic shift when love for and belief in them and their presence is sent their way.

There is another kind of meeting and being together in the silence that can occur apart from that graced by mutual care and respect. John drew my attention to this when he referred, about three years after his passing, to the time mentioned in the last chapter when we were reading the Gospel of St. John and were struck wordless. He asked me to reconstruct those moments and to call up the profound feeling of awe that accompanied them. My understanding is that the words of the Gospel carried us back—or forward—into the realm beyond words from which they came. Moreover, this realm is a place not only of rest—in the sense of taking rest or quietly regrouping between periods of activity—it is a place of continual gestation. John said the awe called forth in both of us helps to hold him to his path on the other side. Furthermore, the recollection was not a one-time thing; the awe *is still* there for him—and for me also. Though I am unable to perceive any of this activity, I believe in the value he ascribes to it and know I, too, feel clearer about and closer to my own path when I am in touch with that state of being.

Among the messages from John from the first six months after he died are some about his passage. Here are three:

> It is a wonderful and terrible thing to realize that death changes nothing—and only Christ can help you make true changes. To ask Him to help you make the changes in your relationship with someone who has died—that is indeed an event! It can change whole configurations of possible events, events yet to come. To ask Christ to mediate always, to ask Him to set you both straight on the path to fruitful collaboration between the living and the dead, that is right and necessary.

❧

> I wait, not so much to answer your questions about me and how I am, but to participate in your questions about the big things, to follow your explorations and discoveries in the spiritual realms and to give them shape on earth in words. The more lively the thoughts and feelings, the more involved I can be both as helper and as friend. Our relationship can continue to grow and change even now. Everyone should remember that when they remember the dead. Could it be that your recent dreams about my physical body as sick and wasting away have to do with views you hold of me that need to be quietly and readily dropped? Are you clinging to something? Are you afraid to step out into the non-physical realms? Examine your own feelings and be willing to let go of unnecessary baggage.

❧

A certain amount of work must be done when you first come over. Call it composting what your life was built around, the thoughts, places, country, race, people you were close to, the work you did... the whole mishmash! You have to compost it all, break yourself down, digest, sift out, see what you are as a result of that last life. There is pain in the process. Joy too. Resolve arises to do better, right what you wronged, be more this, less that. You're familiar with all these thoughts, I reassure you, they're right on!

To know this and enter gladly and fully into it is important. Many don't want to engage with their compost. They're ashamed, afraid, sleepy. For some it takes forever. For those who know, it becomes a labor of love, done with His help.

Yes, He is here: the first born from the dead! Moving among the dead, observing with love their progress, earnestly desiring their awakening. So many are compartmentalized. It is so sad.

Great and wonderful things are going on. Angels are engaged and involved with humanity in ways they weren't before. Barriers are coming down. Hearts are opening. Leaders (on both sides) will have to stop posturing in the face of what's happening. Will have to wake up and put their own humanity on the line. It is true the sacrifices of one can spill out over all and become food/drink for all. Only a few are able to do this. Some, like Mother Teresa, are known; others are not. A life lived in secret in Christ can go a long way toward feeding the world. (11/4/98)

John was as thorough and thoughtful with the life composting he was doing on the other side as he'd been on this side when he worked in his backyard. It took me a while, however, to figure out what was going on. Edward and I were busy with our work starting the school, and that was the primary thing on my mind. I guess I assumed John was mostly focused on that, too. Hadn't he said he was eager to get to the other side in order to be of help? In addition, he was helpful to the degree that I sensed him cheering us on, but there were also other primary things for him.

I first became aware of John's "composting" one evening when we were with a group of friends who had met weekly at his home to read Steiner together. We were in his living room with Carol, and the group was discussing what book to read. This was not quite a year after he'd passed on. I sensed that he not only wanted to hear a specific book, he specially wanted a certain person in the group to hear it. The next week this person suggested he and I have lunch together, and during the meal I realized he was quite upset by a couple of private exchanges he'd had with John before John died. The gist of the matter was that John wanted to hear the grievances.

Less than a week later another person asked to get together to talk, and more stories about John emerged. This happened with three people, and I decided it was not a coincidence. Every time it happened I not only felt John's presence, I felt his sadness. I did not tell any of these people my sense of what was going on, as I didn't think that was called for. I did not sense John trying to talk to them through me, nor did I feel I was being asked to explain anything, or to smooth things over, by saying, for example, that he hadn't been quite himself at the end of his life, or that he had sometimes put ideals before human feelings. John would never have consented to that. I hoped that the airing of hurt, disappointed, and bewildered feelings would clear the air for everyone, but it was obvious some hurts ran deep and could not be given up or transformed in one day, one week, or one month.

Some of these hurts may sound trivial to the reader—
for example, John's suggestions about changing one's way
of working, or one's speech, dress, even one's hair style—
yet the comments went deep, far deeper than he realized.
In the common-day sphere of life he simply didn't know
the power his words had over people. For some, these
words were an affront, an outright criticism of who and
what they were. As a young woman I'd experienced first
hand this tendency in John to want to change or neaten
things up, so I could sympathize with their accounts.
Sometimes, however, I could see how his suggestion
might have helped as, for example, when he told others
to stop drinking or smoking. (He himself had been quite
a smoker as young man.)

Did these stories affect my own view of John? You bet
they did! I'd known all along that he rubbed some people
wrong, but having a lot of ghosts coming out of closets
all at once was a new and totally unexpected experience.
It seems to me that most people, after a person dies, try
instinctively to speak of the good things in that life or
personality. Sometimes it's easy, sometimes not so easy,
but the overall effort is generous. It's as though we know
that someday others will be able to say whatever they
want about us, and we're going to be forced to hear it,
and we're not going to be able to respond to them. Others
are going to have the final say about our lives.

Though ghosts were coming out of closets, and would
continue to emerge for a couple of years, please understand that not everybody was talking in this way. For
every person who complained there were at least four
who spoke of their love for John, their wonderful memories, and how he had influenced their lives. Later I realized that some of those who complained had not really
known him and were going by way of what they had
heard from others.

At first I was flattered that people were taking me into their confidence, then I began to get angry. I was angry at John for being tactless, I was angry at people for not speaking up, being honest, and trying to work through things with him themselves when he was alive, and finally I was angry that everything had to be so complicated. I told John as much. What I received in return stunned me: immense warmth and gratitude because he *wanted* to hear what they had to say, and above all he *wanted* to feel what they felt, not just about him, but because of him.

Let me share three other incidents of this sort.

When I sent in my application to participate in a sixty-mile walk to raise money for breast cancer care and research, I received a list of the names of about twenty-five walkers in my area whom I could contact if I wanted to train with them. While staring at the list and wondering how to decide whom to call, I sensed John pointing at a name. It was the name of a man, also named John, whom I'll call Johnny to make the story easier to follow. Soon Johnny and I were walking together two or three times a week, sometimes with others, sometimes by ourselves. We enjoyed swapping stories as we walked, and one day, when it was just the two of us, Johnny began describing a lecture he'd heard by "a very impressive man." First I sensed John's presence, and then I realized Johnny was talking about John!

The realization gave me goose pimples. Here we were walking along—John, unseen, on my right, listening to Johnny, on my left, describing a talk John had given three or four years earlier.

"He wasn't affiliated with any church or dogma but he knew *exactly* what he thought," Johnny said (or something to this effect). "He believed in God, and God's will, and while I admired him, I wondered how anybody could be so sure."

I could feel John listening intently.

I told Johnny I thought I knew the person he was talking about and gave him John's full name. He stopped, astonished. I told him a bit about our connection to John and John's death.

Johnny said he had wanted to know more about John's thoughts and his faith, and had gotten himself invited for tea one Sunday afternoon. He and John had an interesting conversation. It was evident from the way Johnny used the word "interesting" that the meeting had been that and nothing more.

"So he wasn't helpful?" I asked.

Johnny shrugged. "You know, people like that can be hard on other people, really hard. They come across as *so* arrogant."

We walked on, my arms cool and prickly. John was really straining to hear and to understand.

Maybe ten minutes passed before Johnny stopped again and said, "I want to revise what I said a while back. He was a great man. In his single-mindedness, he was a great man."

A feeling of immense relief washed over me. I believe it was John's relief. Months later, during the actual walk, I told Johnny who had been with us that day. He believed it on the spot and we have, since then, remained good friends. He has also been of much help to us in our work founding a school. Is it too much to say I believe John brought Johnny our way? As I said there were about twenty-five names on that list, yet Johnny's name was the one my attention was drawn to.

Another time, Edward and I were out west visiting a couple we hadn't seen for years. The wife had gone through the Waldorf teacher-training program and had taught at the school when Edward was there. I'd been aware of John's respect for her and her husband when he was alive.

We shared news with our friends and many memories, *good* memories, so I was surprised when we sat down to dinner the last evening and I got the impression John wanted to get to the root of something.

I asked the wife if she had enjoyed working for John. She said yes. Half an hour later out of the blue she began to talk about a difficult moment with him from fifteen years earlier. Then there was another such moment.

It wasn't as though John had been mean, just brusque, and opinionated. His little comments had, however, remained in this proud and artistic woman, just below the surface, for years, festering.

I felt astonishment from John.

Later, after we'd departed from these friends, I tried entering deeper into the astonishment in an effort to understand what it was like for him. He was astonished he had made such callous comments. In the past-life recall he saw his interactions with her and felt her hurt, yet he wanted to hear it all again, as described by her, years later. He was that scrupulous. I believe they both were helped on that occasion.

The third incident—and these incidents occurred about a year apart—happened when I was going to meet a friend for lunch about seventy miles away. Though I had written directions, I realized fifteen minutes before the time I was due to meet my friend that I'd taken a wrong turn and was miles from where I was supposed to be. My very first thought was to find somebody who could phone her for me so she wouldn't be alarmed when I didn't show up.

As I was driving on the heavily used road looking for a service station or some other place with a telephone, I inwardly heard, "Turn left."

I took the first left and found myself on a country road. Puzzled, and certain I wouldn't find a gas station, I slowed almost to a crawl.

At the next intersection I again heard, "Turn left."

I was certain then that John was speaking and leading the way. I also remembered that relatives of John lived in this area and I'd been there once years before. The result was that I wound up at the door of the house where one of his relative's lived! I would never have been able to find this place on my own without an address or a map. She welcomed me, helped me place a phone call to my friend, and invited me to her home for lunch.

I won't talk about John's relationships with his relatives, because that is not my business. I know he loved and admired them. There had been some difficulties, and John wanted to hear right then, and freshly, whatever this person had to say. I can't remember now what was said, but I will always remember the qualities of regret and hope that surrounded this encounter. John's regret that he hadn't done enough during his last twenty years to connect in a loving way with certain members of his family. And his hope was that it was possible. That hope is still there.

By the time this happened—and I moved in a state of wonder all of that day, feeling as though I was acting out a part in a play—I was no longer angry. Or rather, I'd arrived at a place where I knew there was no point in being angry. My anger was irrelevant. It could not really console anyone or help anyone to mend anything. John was not asking me to respond in these situations, I did not hear any words or receive any impressions from him to that effect. So *why*, if I was needed, *was* I needed?

Nothing has been explained to me, and I'll be the first to admit I'm a novice when it comes to offering help to the dead. I do not know this territory the way Rudolf Steiner does. I do not spend whole days praying, remembering the deceased and asking, "What can I do?" (Maybe I should.) Quite simply, I found myself in these situations where people needed to express their negative feelings about John. It was as though the words I'd heard from him for half a year or so after he died were being replaced more and more by *impulses*. There was the impulse of these people to speak, and there was the impulse in me to see these people and listen to what they had to say. I believe John was behind these impulses. If he was pushy about what he believed and longed to achieve when on this side, then, by golly, he could be pushy on the other side too! As I just stated, though, I was not angry. I was in awe—and I remain in awe—at the determination of the man.

I will venture a guess as to why I was needed: the living can act as a catalyst in the life review process of the deceased. It's my impression John not only saw and felt the effects of his personality and his actions on others; he also wanted to do everything possible on earth to speed up the composting. Moreover, he wanted to speed it up not only for his own sake but for the sake of the living, and especially for the sake of the thoughts he loves and serves. If his faith was perceived as arrogance, then he wanted to do whatever he could to shift the gaze of the living from him to the source of his faith. If my presence could be used to remind people of him and to encourage them to open up and share their grievances so they could move beyond them, he would call on me to be there. I'm sure he has called on others on this side also to be of help to him.

If the thought of the dead using the living to help them neaten up their affairs is bothersome to the reader, then I'm far indeed from conveying a fact that underlies this book: the urges behind many of our actions and thoughts— both good and not so good—are implanted in us by the dead. We're just not aware of it. When we can awaken to this then we'll not only begin to work with them, we'll also begin to see that we have the freedom to choose the impulses and ideals we want to live by.

When Carol died, four years after John, the house they'd lived in for over twenty years was put on the market. In the rush to clean it out, about a dozen boxes of their belongings wound up in our basement. I assumed the boxes were filled with books and magazines, but one evening when Edward was away at a conference and I was watching television, I found out otherwise.

In the middle of the news broadcast I sensed John's presence in the doorway of the room. I'd never connected with him while watching TV, and was startled, the more so because he seemed agitated.

I got up, turned off the machine, and *knew* he wanted me to go into the basement. Once there I found myself surveying the mountain of boxes. I *knew* he was in search of something in one of the boxes, but which box? After a few minutes of waiting I felt myself being directed to one in the back, beneath two others. When I finally got this box out in the open and was able to look inside I discovered stacks of letters. All of them had been written to him around the time he had been asked to leave the Waldorf School, more than twenty years earlier.

This may sound mawkish but I felt, quite literally, as though I'd opened Pandora's Box as sad, disappointed, hostile and discouraged feelings rushed out. I was moved to tears when I saw the familiar handwriting of people I knew or had known when we were at the Waldorf School.

I started to open one of the letters and got a very clear, "*No!*" John did not want the letters read, he wanted them destroyed.

I lugged the box upstairs, got a pair of scissors, and another clear, "*No!*" came through. Everything was to be burned. It took me a couple of hours to shred the letters into the fire in the fireplace. When the job was done, a sweet sense of relief and of gratitude washed over me.

I thought maybe this was the end of my involvement in John's composting, but about eight months later, I woke one morning to another request. The gist of this one was that he wanted, in my presence, to review several decisions he'd made during his lifetime. They were decisions that had deeply affected others, had altered outer events, and had caused quite a bit of anguish.

For the first time I hesitated. My inner reaction was, "More? And *this*.... I don't think I'm equal to this one."

When I assisted John in his review work the feelings of the others *and* his feelings about their feelings could be experienced. I felt their anger and his shame. Or their disappointment and his disappointment. Or their relief and his elation. The distinctions between them, him, and me fell away briefly. When there was anger and pain, I didn't think about them any more than you think, "I'm angry" or "This is painful" when you're furious at a person and smarting at a comment that person has made. You're *in* the anger or the pain, there's no room for thought, except maybe as, "Damn!" or "Ouch!" This can be exhausting. For me, this is another reason I need to call on Christ before entering into communications with the dead. *Awakening* literally means waking to the presence of the dead *in* us rather than as separate from us, as we're accustomed to experiencing people on this side. Christ knows how much of that I can take at a given time.

Above all, I hesitated to help John when reviewing decisions he'd made because I honestly did not feel equal to the possibility in his request that he had made wrong decisions. Some of his decisions had influenced us directly. If they were wrong, did that mean we had made wrong turns also and were on the wrong course in our own lives?

The possibility terrified me. Everything—past, present, the other side and this side, faith and doubt, love and fear—seemed too close. For the third time in my life I shut the door, so to speak, to the other side, and immersed myself in everyday work.

I knew I was letting John down, was not being a true friend, and I was ashamed. At the same time I was driven to do, to act, to involve myself in the round of everyday activities. I could see plenty of things in front of me that needed to be done, too, and that was reassuring. But my heart was only half involved. When I ignore the other side, life seems flat. It loses a dimension. It's as though I become color blind, and I know I'm responsible but, hey, I can still see, so I'm just going to keep going.

I mention all this because I think it's important not only to know that we *can* close the door—indeed, it is our right to be able to close it—but because the closing may actually be necessary. When we're hungry we seek food, when we're weary we seek rest, and when we're frankly overwhelmed, even if we have called on Christ for help, what's wrong with stepping back? I've learned since then the importance of not forcing things, of being able to shift my attention to other things so my ability to be attentive is, in fact, replenished. I've learned, too, the fact that the outer *and* inner worlds need to be protected from *me*! No matter how lofty I may believe my intentions to be, when I rush I may, unknowingly, be out of sync. There really *is* a right time and a wrong time to act.

Thus it happened that I missed the connection with John, and when I opened the door again almost a month later he was still there with the same request. By this time I had more or less moved beyond my own, personal anxiety. I could see with my everyday eyes that decisions Edward and I had made, which had been influenced by decisions John had made, had borne fruit. True, the school we set out to start before he died had only lasted two years, but it prepared the way for another attempt that was, right then, beginning and gaining in strength. If I had consented to

help him while I was still upset I might have been a burden
rather than a help.

Curiously, this review was not what I expected. There
were no faces, no names, no visual replay of events. To
speak metaphorically, it was as though John went alone
every day for about a week into a closed courtroom and
I waited outside and held him in prayer. I felt he was in a
state of strain, laboring to sort through and smooth out
some very deep matters. All I could do was stand firm in
the belief that, in every instance I knew of, he had acted
from out of the highest in himself. It was as though I was
repeating the words he had lived by, saying them both to
and for him:

> One cannot say, "Of what use to me are the per-
> cepts to follow purely the laws of the True, when I
> am mistaken perhaps as to what is the True?" What
> matters is the striving and the attitude to it. Even a
> man who is mistaken has in his very striving after
> the True a force that diverts him from the wrong
> path. If he is mistaken, this force guides him to the
> right paths.

And, "Love God and do what you will."

This ordeal occurred during the Holy Nights at Christ-
mastime. It was over one morning after the new year had
begun. For me it was a bit of an anticlimax. It was as
though he came out of the courtroom a different man,
drained of himself, yet radiating equanimity. And nothing was said, but I felt his relief and gratitude. I wanted
with my mind to "know" more, to understand better what
had happened, but sensed in my heart this had been a test
for me as much as for him. Would I stand by him, would
I remain his friend even if the judge within had said his

decisions were wrong? Yes! Because his belief in the True has become my belief in and love for the True.

John's life review may still be going on, but in my own dealings with him I'm not aware of it. I've received the impression many times of his interest in what we're doing, and there's nothing overbearing in this interest. Edward and I have both, on several occasions, wondered if John and other dear departed friends have been behind various events as *exactly* the right people, and *exactly* the right places, have appeared when needed in our work on this side, as evidenced in the example given earlier of the man named Johnny. I've also received impressions of John meeting others "over there," studying, traveling, and being involved in work he hasn't yet shared with me. When I ask him how he is, I often receive inner impressions of smiles and of clasped hands raised high in greeting.

I am going to close this chapter with words John jotted on a piece of paper that fluttered out of one of his journals shortly after I began thinking about the matter of waking up to our connections with the dead. These words have been on my desk throughout the writing, and best express the mood of this endeavor:

Love & Freedom
Love is that creative condition in which in one's
    ignorance one yet knows,
  and despite one's helplessness yet accomplishes.

𝒜FTERWORD

A FRIEND WHO READ this manuscript in the early stages
said, "What you say is helpful and reassuring, but
what can we do to awaken to the dead?"

There was an urgency to his words, the same urgency
I often heard in John when he was alive, and now sometimes feel coming from him. Perhaps John was speaking
through this friend, perhaps not. In a way it doesn't matter, but the question matters.

What can we do to awaken to the dead?

A couple of thoughts come to me when I contemplate
this question.

First, I think it helps to be aware of the ideas one holds
concerning dying, death, and the dead. Those ideas may
have been handed down by one's parents; shaped by the
religious domination one grew up in or later joined; or
passed on by friends, mentors, or teachers. One may need
to dig around a bit to find them and may, in fact, be surprised by what one discovers.

A woman I met years ago admitted that her picture of
life after death had been formed by a chance reading in
the dentist's office. It was a book excerpt in a magazine by
a person who'd had a near-death experience. The woman
held on to the thoughts in this excerpt after her sister and
mother died. No one in her family believed in life after
death and, for a long time she wondered if her attraction
in what she'd read was a form of denial of the deaths in

her family. Finally she decided she *wanted* to believe in life after death regardless of what others said or thought. She said she felt incredibly happy after making that decision and added that it seemed as though her sister and mother were right there with her, smiling and laughing. This sense of closeness was with her for some time, but even after it faded the certainty remained. By then she was reading whatever she could get her hands on, about near-death experiences and life after death.

This goes to show that, whatever their source, the ideas we hold may open or close doors. Becoming aware of the ideas can aid or speed up the opening. This is surely true not only for us in relationship with those who have died but also for us personally. It seemed to me when I worked at Hospice that part of the pain patients were experiencing was due to fear of death. How dramatically different one can feel, physically as well as emotionally, when one is open to the possibility that death is a transition we all make, that it need not be ugly or hurtful, that it may actually be a release and the beginning of a whole new chapter. Furthermore, if we die in a state of fear or confusion we may well find ourselves still in that state on the other side. In this way we can become a "needy" dead person, neither there nor here, a kind of dead weight (no pun intended) on both those we've left behind and those on the other side. I believe there are "homeless" dead souls hanging around everywhere for various reasons. They may be plain bewildered, lonely, unable to let go of people or situations on this side, or uncertain as to how to disengage from their physical bodies. I've sensed but not communicated directly with this population because I don't yet know enough to offer my services. There is a great need for knowledge of and work in this area. Discovering what makes it possible for one to die a "good" death is surely a major step we can all take in this direction.

While growing up, I was aware of my parent's disinterest in or avoidance of the subject; that my maternal grandmother believed in reincarnation; and that, on a World War I battlefield, my paternal grandfather, an Episcopal priest, had experienced a crisis of faith, from which he never recovered. (He told me about it when I was twelve.) I was not under any pressure from anyone to believe or disbelieve any point of view. This is not the case for everyone, and I'm immensely grateful for the freedom of thought and belief I've known all my life.

Are one's ideas about death shaped in freedom or compulsion? I think that's a question worth asking oneself, and not just once but many times.

One may also acquire one's ideas by way of one's own experiences. As I try to show in part one of this book, most of my experiences of people on the other side "happened" to me. When I had them I didn't automatically conclude, "I believe in life after death." For me it was just a curious fact that affected me in sometimes pleasant, other times unpleasant, ways. I'm sure experiences of these sorts "happen" to many people, children especially. Thus I didn't really begin to wake to the meaning of my experiences until I came into contact with others who took the time to articulate not only what had happened to them, but what they'd discovered. (Following this afterword, I have included a list of books that have helped me.)

There are a couple of implications here. We can be asleep to the deeper meanings and possibilities in the experiences we are having. Simply having experiences doesn't mean we're awake in them or to them, doesn't necessarily mean we can interpret them in a valid way. Again—this cannot be repeated too often—we *need* each other in order to awaken. My discoveries not only add to yours; yours also add to mine. I'm referring here to all of humanity, and on both sides. We don't wake up on the other side once and for all in the same way we wake every morning. Waking up to the other side is an ongoing adventure, a quest, and a process, not a one-time event. I also think the waking is different for each person. One person may leap into momentary wakefulness and then slip back into slumber. For another it may happen slowly, step by step.

It's my impression that the dead also sleep, wake, and sleep again. As you may have noticed from the accounts I've shared, one can, upon crossing over, find oneself in pretty much the same place one was in at the time of death. An example is the suicide discovering he's still stuck in his unhappy situation and there's no escaping it or himself. Yet I've been told that change and growth *are* possible on the other side. Events of all kinds happen there also, and one may meet helpers and teachers whom one did not know when on this side.

This brings me to the second thought I'd like to share.

I believe our ability to awaken to the dead depends to a large degree on our ability to learn another language. This language is, in the book *Staying Connected*, described by Rudolf Steiner as the language of the heart:

> We find our way into a language that is not at all
> formed according to earthly conditions, but is rather
> a language arising from feelings, from the heart. It is
> a kind of language of the heart. (p. 207)

My understanding of this is that, when our love for those who has gone on is greater than it was while they were still on this side, when it becomes love for their very essence, we find we haven't "lost" them when they die. We know their essence will always be with us, *in* us, and we open to the language of the heart.

I hope I've been able to show in this book the manner in which I, myself, hear and converse with the dead in this language. Perhaps it bears repeating that I usually hear the dead soul within my thoughts, feelings, and impulses. (I say "usually" because there have been times when I've known a dead person to be present in an external way. This happens with people I either did not know or did not know well when they were alive, as in the case of Tim in part one of this book. I have also seen apparitions that I have not been able to connect with or identify.) Recognizing the thoughts or feelings coming from the dead person means knowing that these thoughts and feelings are not my own, even though I may be in perfect accord with them, may, to speak metaphorically, feel as though I'm performing a duet with them.

Sympathy and empathy, shared feelings of interest, support, pleasure, awe, happiness, contentment, yearning, and respect are all a part of the "vocabulary" of this language of the heart. For example, the dead person can speak within as a longing for contact. One can find oneself missing this person, maybe wanting to look at their photograph, touch or wear an article of clothing that belonged to them, be in a place they loved, or read a book they enjoyed. One may hope nobody on this side notices one's strange behavior! It's easy to assume it's just us missing them when in fact the longing, the impulse to connect, though it may be mutual, may first have been sent forth by them.

There is a fundamental difference between this language of the heart and language as we know it here in everyday life. On this side we normally think of language as meaning words, and we often use words without being fully in them. Spoken or written, we use words as symbols, signposts, indicators, and means to an end. This doesn't work for the language of the heart. This language has to be *alive*, has to be *active*, has to be fully and truly *meant* if it is to be heard and shared. It has to be created anew, out of feelings, thoughts, and impulses, *every* time it is used. The language of the heart also encompasses far more than words. It can be heard in music or other sounds, read in pictures or colors, clothed in scent. I've sensed dead souls expressing gladness for being with their living friends during moments of prayer through the delicate aroma of cooking bread, when no baking was occurring on the physical plane. I believe this is similar to Mary making her presence known to her followers through the scent of roses. Furthermore, I believe there are no limits to the possible expressiveness of this language. The joy of it is in the aliveness with which it moves among and between souls, and that need not necessarily mean it only occurs between two at a time.

The language of the heart can be extremely sensuous in that the receptivity of the physical senses may be heightened when one is using it. The world can look brighter. Every object and person can seem to shine. Yet the language of the heart can be felt to be quite apart from the ordinary workings of the physical senses because it is understood and responded to almost entirely *within*. For example, when I hear words within, thoughts often form within me in response to them, and replies to these thoughts can come even as the thoughts are forming! It could be said that the language of the heart is the language of love, but that really means nothing unless you are experiencing it. When you're using it you're *in* it, in the same way that one can know oneself to be *in* love with another person. (In this instance I mean the term to encompass far more than purely romantic involvement.) One may also tend to regard love as an emotion devoid of thought, and this language of the heart is certainly not devoid of thought. The exchange of thoughts can be so close and immediate with the one who has passed over, it bypasses words. Yet still it is a language. We get a taste of it on this side when we are close to a person and simultaneously share the same thoughts and feelings.

To return to the example given earlier of longing to be with the one who has gone on: the longing, though it may vary in intensity, has to be fresh in order for communication to occur. Can one call up longing within in order to connect with someone on the other side? I have. At the same time I've received the impression this must be done with tact, even as relationships on this side require tact. Once a friend on the other side greeted me with: "I love you too... and I'm busy right now." Can one imagine that someone who has died is longing for one, while in fact one is wallowing in personal loss? I suppose so.

Grief often plays a large role in the development of the language of the heart. I use the word "often" rather than "always" here because there are occasions when people are unable to find their way in and through grief. They're so stunned they've retreated to a point of paralysis within themselves. Though going through the motions of living, they're actually unable to relate to anybody, living or dead, in a meaningful way. In the positive experience—and you may quite naturally wonder how there can be any "positive" thing about grief—grief can lead one beyond the usual boundaries of one's life and consciousness, even though the condition may feel as though one has fallen out of time and is perilously close to insanity. All that is near and familiar suddenly falls away. This loosening can change the way one perceives things on this side; what formerly irritated one can seem silly, inconsequential. Small, generous gestures made by others can, quite unexpectedly, call forth immense gratitude and tears. An hour spent remembering another or reading to that person can seem like no more than ten minutes. When this kind of expansion occurs, the language of the heart grows and changes, in the same way that conversations between friends grow and change as people get to know one another. The "tone" of grief may evolve from raw, to sharp and bitter, to less sharp, to bitter-sweet. These "tones," these feelings, are an important part of the changing vocabulary of the language of the heart. For what is happening is not happening to you alone, the one who has died is also going through new territory and soul expansion.

Curiously enough I myself find it helpful to employ words in order to work toward proficiency in this language of the heart. For example, when I feel the longing to connect with someone on the other side I may attempt to express this longing more and more succinctly by way of written or spoken words. I might, for example, start writing a letter to the person on the other side, and even before it is completed I may know we're both "online." The act of trying to put things in words, the *right* words, is not easy. What comes out can sound sentimental, presumptuous, even contrived. When this happens I hear I'm off-key, and may stop and try again later, or try to push on past the lack of clarity or faintheartedness that blocks the way. I've also composed verses and found they could be used more than once to help make the transition to the language of the heart. Here is one verse that helped me to establish a sense of ritual when I sought to connect with John, and served as an aid for several years:

> Now I shut this door
> and open the other—
> Now I turn from
> this thought headed out there,
> that feeling churning in here
> to the ray of light
> that makes all visible
> though it cannot itself be seen.

Lord Christ be with us
Lord Christ watch over us,
allow us to meet
and converse in Your Name.

Now I turn to the warmth of your being;
the remembered eyes,
one darker and deeper than the other,
the remembered smiles, words, exchanges,
the shared trust and hope,
the kinship in service.

It is easy to enter
into the re-membering
fresh and close as today.
But I sense you waiting,
wordless and waiting,
as though you've had enough
of snapshots in an album,
as though the memories have become
too much food in the stomach.

The angel needs us lean and true.

Lord Christ be with us.
Lord Christ watch over us,
allow us to meet
and converse in Your Name.

I have also found verses in the Psalms or by Steiner,
Rilke, Rumi, Blake and Keats helpful when trying to make
the shift from ordinary, everyday speech to the language
of the heart. Sometimes I only need to read one line of
Rilke and I've made the adjustment. It is as though I'm

able to hitch a ride into another dimension by yielding to the powers, the feelings, and the music in their words.

To return to the question: What can one do to awaken?

I am not able, in response, to offer a program, a series of exercises or meditations, a surefire way to enable one to wake to the presence of loved ones on the other side. I do, however, believe that asking is the first step. For I've found that *every* question that rises up from deep down within has the potential to become a moving force that can carry one, through both sleepy and wakeful times, *exactly* where one needs to go.

Even a question as simple as, "Are we connecting?" can take you somewhere. Don't throw it out in an impatient way, ask it in the morning when you get up, ask it when you look at the photo of your dear dead friend or relative, ask it when you go to bed at night. Then hold to a listening, waiting attitude, an attitude that creates the necessary space within you for the answer to come. Don't make the mistake of predetermining how *you* think or want it to come, because you may not recognize it for what it is when it does come. As I've tried to show in this book, answers may come from without as well as from within, in the form of meetings, encounters, events, words spoken by others.

Be open, too, to the possibility that the answers to your questions may not come for weeks, months, even years. Don't let disappointment get the better of you if nothing is forthcoming. As I've said earlier, there is such a thing as "right timing." One of the biggest, reoccurring tests for me in the matter of communicating with the other side has been learning to wait—and wait—and wait!

I'd like to stress once again the importance of questions coming from our innermost, not out of mere curiosity. On this side we can pretend to be interested in another person when we're talking with him, while our mind is elsewhere. This doesn't work with the dead; we must be present, just as the language we use with them has to be immediate, arising directly from the heart. There have been times when I've known my questions are—so to speak—going to bounce off the door and land back in my lap. Questions like, "Oh, by the way, have you got any sense of who's going to win the next presidential election?" or, "Can you see me doing everything—like brushing my hair? Or taking that extra cookie from the cookie jar?"

As one asks questions, and answers appear, as one moves with the "questing" forces of the question, waking occurs and the language of the heart comes alive in one. Furthermore, these questions we ask from the depths of ourselves may be coming to us from the dead. We may think *we* are asking the question, when, in fact, the dead soul has stirred, dropped, or planted, the question in us. The best example I can give of this is a question that has come up periodically in my life: "Am I doing what I'm meant to be doing?" I don't want to sound like I'm giving others permission to be dissatisfied with their lives but I do believe, for myself, that different souls on the other side have—through this question—lead me to different places and different jobs. This question can come to be heard within as a loving, "Are you doing what you're meant to be doing, what you really want to be doing?" and "Are you doing all you know you are capable of doing?"

To summarize: be attentive to the questions that both flutter lightly and burn within. Attempt to answer them as truthfully as you are able, and new questions will arise as you seek the answers. I've never particularly liked the word *process*; it makes me think of things being thrown into a blender, but here it comes closest to what I'm trying to describe. Connecting with the dead is, very definitely, an ongoing process.

Recently I woke on night around 3 AM, looked out the window and was delighted, after many cloudy, rainy days to be able to see the stars. The heavens were truly abloom! This thought came to me in a rush: the dead need us to be their stars on earth. We enable them to see in the midst of all the clouds of confusion, hatred, and sorrow on earth. We must not become clouded, we must let our spirits shine for them so they can see how they can connect with us, and what they must do to come back and help this world.

How are we doing that?

How can we do it?

I'll leave those questions with you.

May you know many wonder-filled awakenings.

SUGGESTED READING

BOOKS THAT HAVE helped me find my way toward more wakeful wakefulness:

Anonymous, *Bridge over the River: After Death Communications of a Young Artist Who Died in World War I*, Great Barrington, MA: Anthroposophic Press, 1974.

Barker, Elsa, written through the hand of, *Letters from the Afterlife: A Guide to the Other Side*, Hillsboro, OR: Beyond Words Publishing, 2004.

Brock, Ira, *Dying Well: Peace and Possibilities at the End of Life*, New York: Riverhead Books, 1998.

Lonsdale, Ellias and Theanna, *The Book of Theanna: In the Lands that Follow Death*, New York: Frog, Ltd., 1995.

Moody, Raymond A., *Life after Life: The Investigation of a Phenomenon—Survival of Bodily Death,* San Francisco: HarperSanFrancisco, 2001.

Richie, George, with Elizabeth Sherrill, *Return from Tomorrow*, Grand Rapids, MI: Fleming H. Revell, 1978.

Sparrow, G. Scott, *Witness to His Return*, Virginia Beach, VA: ARE Press, 1991.

Steiner, Rudolf, *Staying Connected: How to Continue Your Relationships with Those Who Have Died* (selected talks and meditations), Great Barrington, MA: Anthroposophic Press, 1999. Christopher Bamford's introduction and chapter comments are also of great help.

——, *Life Beyond Death: Selected Lectures*, London: Rudolf Steiner Press, 1995.